The Maverick Paradox

The Secret Power Behind Successful Leaders

Judith Germain

Copyright © 2017 Judith Germain
www.maverickparadox.com

All rights reserved, including the right to reproduce this book, or portions thereof in any form. No part of this text may be reproduced, transmitted, downloaded, decompiled, reverse engineered, or stored, in any form or introduced into any information storage and retrieval system, in any form or by any means, whether electronic or mechanical without the express written permission of the author.

For permissions email: contact@maverickparadox.com

The views expressed in this work are solely those of the author and do not necessarily reflect the views of the publisher, and the publisher hereby disclaims any responsibility for them.

ISBN: 978-1-326-99341-2

First Edition

PublishNation
www.publishnation.co.uk

Table of Contents

Preface		iv
Acknowledgements		viii
Prologue		1
Part 1	**How successful leaders think**	5
Chapter 1	The Maverick Paradox	7
Chapter 2	The Maverick Mindset	44
Part 2	**The competencies of successful leaders**	79
Chapter 3	Maverick (KEY) Capabilities	81
Chapter 4	Maverick (STONE) Capabilities	110
Part 3	**The use of power by successful leaders**	129
Chapter 5	Harnessing maverick power	131
Chapter 6	Maverick leaders	165
Epilogue		203
About the Author		208

Preface

Successful leadership in an ever-shifting landscape isn't easy. Finding your place in the world has become increasingly difficult as the century gets older. The old staples aren't stable anymore and we are no longer sure of the old certainties. Things must change and the time for a new type of leader is upon us.

Not only do we expect individuals to lead, we insist that the companies that 'serve us' also show true leadership as well. A new type of (maverick) leadership made perfect for this century.

Sadly, the world is slow to wake up to this fact. Leadership has become a byword for control and companies have disempowered individuals from realising that they can be leaders in their own sphere of influence. There is no need to revert to companies for permission.

Leadership is hard and successful leadership requires courage. People are more cynical and less trusting. Never before have we needed to trust our leaders and the institutions they represent. It's criminal that we struggle to find an inspiring voice willing to conduct meaningful challenge and be worthy of our trust.

Within this need lies the maverick paradox.

I've never lost a maverick

Whilst working in Senior Management and HR, it was all too clear to me that there were serious mismatches between (a) stated goals and results and (b) stated company culture and management values. This caused me significant cognitive dissonance so I used my influence to challenge the status quo to bring forth change.

The only places that I've worked in, were ones that had significant challenge. In those places, there would always be an Extreme Maverick breaking every rule known to man. I found that opinion was divided about them, should they be saved or not?

I became the go to person, the one that could harness the power and talent of the maverick. I found it perplexing that others could not understand the mavericks in their organisation. For example, once the Socialised Maverick had solved the challenge that they had been hired to resolve, their managers would constrict what they were allowed to do. This meant that there was insufficient challenge within the role for them.

A maverick needs challenge and influence like oxygen.

Judith, the Socialised Maverick!

Eventually I recognised that *I* was a Socialised Maverick and that my desire was to work with other mavericks to enhance the impact that they had on the world and reduce the negative consequences that some mavericks were inflicting on others. I realised that from childhood, I've been haunted by two questions (a) *'Why do people do that?'* and (b) *'how can I get what I want?'* ('luckily when I was 17, I started working for a Socialised Maverick that helped me amend that question to *'how can I get what I want, ethically?'* This changed the course of my life. A lot of mavericks do not get that early intervention. I want to help mavericks become truly powerful and choose to work for the greater good).

These two questions have led me to my experimental, practical, and theoretical study of mavericks, (those that are wilfully independent). I have spent close to 30 years trying to interpret and enhance the results of my personal study, to improve leadership within individuals and organisations. I began a study into many areas, such as leadership, social psychology, NLP, Social and Emotional Intelligence; to name a few. When I was working in the HR profession, I added behavioural aspects of human nature to my study. A keen modeller of behaviour as well as having the ability to be able to test my hypotheses enabled me to truly understand the nature of mavericks and how to influence them.

I've tested my theories and bespoke solutions with the hundreds of leaders and organisations I've worked with. Sometimes the best research is in the field and eventually I discovered that there were two types of mavericks. Socialised and Extreme, similar in behaviour, different in intention.

It truly saddens me that despite the last 100 years of leadership study, man is no further forward. Mankind seemingly confused with the notion that, before you can get someone to follow you, you need to be worthy of being followed.

I am a hopeful pragmatist that believes that one day we will live in a world where the truly powerful strives for the greater good. Where every person is a maverick leader, inspired to do the right thing, regardless of the consequences. My mission is to inspire all individuals to want to create that world and to enjoy living in it.

This is my guide to understanding the Maverick Paradox, the secret power behind successful leaders. I provide you with the blueprint to becoming a successful leader. In this book, you will:

- Discover the 5 maverick attributes all 'natural leaders' possess
- Develop a success mindset
- Master the 8 maverick capabilities that all successful leaders demonstrate
- Enhance and extend your influence by utilising the 3 key power bases
 Become a transformational leader by deploying the Maverick DRIVEN Leadership™ Methodology

It will be easier for you to understand mavericks and learn the best ways to make sure that their impact is positive. You will have gained a deeper understanding of why Socialised Mavericks present the best model of leadership and why the toxicity of Extreme Mavericks don't.

Whilst reading this book it is important to remember the following:

- The gender for Extreme Mavericks will always be male
- The gender for Socialised Mavericks can be either male or female. If female, I'm only referring to an Alpha Female
- The gender of Maverick Behaviourists can be either male or female
- Elsewhere in the book, I use the common grammatical construct of referring to 'he', when I could be equally referring to the male or female gender

Now, please continue reading to discover the secret power behind successful leaders …

Acknowledgements

I would like to thank my first readers Simon Phillips, Julian Mead, Annabel Kaye, and Alex Stables for challenging me; and giving me a compelling reason to make changes to this book. I and this book are better for it, and I'm truly grateful for your time and encouragement.

Prologue

HR: We are going to have to discipline John. This can't go on, he's upset Janey again and I'm fed up of having her crying in my office day after day.

This is bullying and it has to stop. What are you going to do about it?

Manager: Look I know that John can be insensitive at times, but he means well. It's just that he doesn't suffer fools gladly and Janey's work has been slipping ...

HR: That's no excuse ...

Manager: I know, I know... what am I going to do though? The customer loves him and the Sales Director thinks he's wonderful. You do know that he has outsold everyone in the company, every year for the last 4 years? I can't discipline him just because he makes someone cry occasionally. What would I do if he leaves?

HR: So, what are you suggesting?

The above conversation and others like it are commonplace in companies, much to the frustration of HR departments everywhere.

Over the many years that I've worked with mavericks, I've observed that their multi-faceted nature can often be perceived as an enigma. Their managers struggle to know how to harness the secret power that they possess and their friends have a fierce loyalty, and sometimes fear of them.

Further analysis shows that there are two types of maverick, Socialised and Extreme; which react in different ways to stimuli. They are almost two sides of the same maverick coin, although one type is highly toxic and has the capability to destroy the world if left to their own devices. The other is a catalyst of beneficial challenge to the status quo.

Mavericks can influence or manipulate situations and people to achieve what they want. They are observant and notice small nuances or changes in behaviour which they use to their advantage. Unlike Socialised Mavericks, Extreme Mavericks tend to manipulate rather than influence. This often causes havoc and bad feeling across an entire organisation. The disruption can lead to 'the management' being too scared to rein in the maverick's excessive behaviour and allow the maverick to become highly successful, despite causing mayhem along the way.

Having a poor leadership cadre can and will ruin companies and lives.

It is common to see managers that tend to be inflexible in their leadership style. These managers have often chosen a style that they like, which they then try to apply to everyone and every situation that they come across.

The solution to both poor leadership and poor performance from your workforce is to encourage more managers and employees to become maverick leaders. Any individual can learn how to become one, if sufficiently motivated. Being a maverick leader is not dependent on having a formal role of authority (e.g. manager). Maverick leadership is a way of life not an organisational formal process.

The plight of the maverick has always fascinated me and during my career I've been bemused as to why people have struggled so much to understand and anticipate the maverick's moods and motivations. Maverick behaviour seemed so perfectly obvious to me, although it took many years for me to realise that I too was a maverick. This was because like many people I believed that there was only one type of maverick. The Extreme Maverick, and I knew that the behavioural traits of this maverick were unlike my own.

It was only after studying maverick behaviour, motivation, and capabilities, did I come to the realisation that there was more than one type. It comes with great relief that I can declare:

I'm a socialised maverick, wilfully independent, not only in personality but in behaviour also.

Mavericks are often misunderstood with their motives misinterpreted, which can lead to disastrous results in the workplace or an individual's psyche, especially if they are subject to an Extreme Maverick's ire. To understand how all types of maverick wield their secret power, you need to be aware of how mavericks think, the capabilities that they have and their likely mode of operation.

I have found it is interesting to note how an individual can transverse the Maverick Continuum [1] ™ and whether an Extreme Maverick can be 'saved' or whether the intricacies of their maverick personality will continually hamper their success.

Maverick leadership is not restricted to those working in organisations, it is applicable to all who aspire to be truly powerful, who want to challenge the status quo; to create a world that they want to live, work and play in. To be maverick, is to be a rule breaking game changer. The only question left to answer, is whether the maverick is going to create a world we all want to live in or recreate it in their own image, for their own benefit.

There is one thing that we can be clear about, is that whichever path the game changing maverick catalyst chooses, he will not be short of loyal followers prepared to follow him to the ends of the earth to deliver his vision to an often unsuspecting audience.

---

[1] Maverick Continuum™ - Judith Germain 2013

Part 1

How successful leaders think

1. The Maverick Paradox

> "He who confronts the paradoxical exposes himself to reality"
> – Friedrich Durrenmatt

If you stopped someone in the street and asked them what a maverick was, they would probably pause a moment, smile and say 'Tom Cruise in Top Gun'. If you asked them to describe a maverick at work they would probably frown, describe a man that is arrogant, blunt, offensive, and good at his job.

It's a dichotomy that both impressions or perceptions can be true. It can be confusing, are we supposed to *like* or *dislike* the maverick?

The maverick paradox is when, *people demand that mavericks change the world, and then hates them when they do.*

Mavericks could be described as people that combine contradictory qualities and are therefore paradoxical in nature. Most mavericks are an enigma and as such are often misunderstood, especially when it comes to interpreting what they are thinking and the reasons why they are doing something. Therefore, people are often surprised when I mention that there is more than one type of maverick, with each type presenting different behaviours, motivations, and varying levels of morality! There is also some surprise when I explain that maverick behaviour can be learnt, and can become an asset in the workplace.

Not all mavericks are created equal although all mavericks share a certain commonality amongst themselves.

Since 2005 I've defined a maverick as someone who is *'wilfully independent'*. This definition always makes me smile because in my imagination the maverick is standing there, looking angelic, with a smirk on his face and more than a hint of devilment in his behaviour.

You never quite know what he is going to do, you do know however that it's going to be interesting!

Films such as Top Gun and Maverick! have helped to popularise the maverick paradox; although they tend to be one sided in their nature. This is because they only show the reckless behaviour and the 'devil don't care' attitude of the maverick. This perceived 'maverick' nature doesn't bode well in the work environment. Individuals that refuse to follow rules and don't get on with their co-workers, tend to get labelled as a 'maverick' by unenlightened colleagues and managers. Whilst at times this might be an accurate diagnosis (that the person is a maverick), often it just describes a 'poor' employee who should be subject to performance management measures! More often or not HR departments and managers are unable to tell the difference between these two types of people (poor performers and mavericks) and they often apply the wrong type of intervention in which to bring about a desirable change of behaviour in the individual.

Interestingly, most people secretly like the idea of being a maverick. In their view, a maverick is a dashing rebel, who fights authority, and does what they like with no consequences. It is easy to see why this perception of a maverick is appealing to many.

This 'type' or more accurately perception of a maverick, is lauded by most, even though their actual behaviour is, perhaps, selfish, and self-serving. Believing in this idea of an untouchable maverick often means when a 'real-life' maverick confronts people, the maverick is given too much freedom, too much fear and too much deference. This is neither good for the work or the home environment.

It can also be dangerous to the maverick.

I have often been asked to describe what a maverick looks like, usually because people are keen to know whether their idea of a maverick matches up to how a maverick has been portrayed in a book or a film. It probably will not surprise you, when I say that films and books tend to present a rather one-dimensional character; usually dashing, rebellious, and an extraverted risk taker. Whilst these fictional characters often exhibit maverick tendencies or behaviours, they are not the definitive answer to the question, 'what does a maverick look like?'

Type of Maverick Personality	
Socialised Maverick	Extreme Maverick
Male/Alpha Female	Male
Can harness maverick power	Exploits maverick power
Influences others	Manipulates others
Believes in objective truth	Believes in relative truth
Will seek to influence compliance, ethically	Will punish harshly for non-compliance
Will work on character to be trusted and trustworthy	Not concerned with being trustworthy, happy to be trusted
Likely to be highly ethical	Likely to be highly unethical
Will seek co-operation	Will seek competition
Considers the moral dimension	Unconcerned with the moral dimension

© **Maverick Personality Types – Judith Germain 2016**

Unsurprisingly, mavericks are usually male or a high Alpha female, regardless of whether they are extraverted or introverted. It is important to note that female mavericks are not usually treated with the same deference or leniency that male mavericks attract. This is often because people expect and accept men to be assertive, self-confident and to have an all-consuming passion for what they want. When a woman acts like this she is believed to be going against her 'nurturing nature' and is usually denigrated.

I believe this is the reason that there are more socialised female mavericks than extreme female mavericks in the world today. The world will not tolerate extreme women, so maverick women have adapted and have become Socialised Mavericks.

Alpha females are interesting because they do not always demonstrate Alpha behaviours in all circumstances. They may be 'Alpha' at work and 'Beta' at home or vice versa. However, when I'm describing a woman with a maverick personality I'm talking about an Alpha female who presents her 'Alpha' traits and behaviours in all circumstances, whatever she is doing, wherever she is. She is likely to be the leader of the group and will nurture the group by starting conversations and smoothing over disagreements. The Alpha female can be described as 'the life and soul of the party' and/or 'Queen Bee'. Sometimes at the same event by different people!

The Alpha maverick female is a confident natural leader who knows what she wants, embracing change and risk, and is often misunderstood.

Unlike male mavericks, Alpha female mavericks tend to be less extreme and become Socialised Mavericks almost immediately. Socialised Mavericks are mavericks that have learnt or are learning how to harness their maverick power. They are no longer extreme in their nature, nor are they compliant. The best way to describe a Socialised Maverick is to say that they have learnt to influence others rather than manipulate them. The Socialised Maverick considers how others are feeling and the best way for the maverick to achieve what they desire, in a way that the other person can readily accept. The Socialised Maverick does not want to harm the other person and will take reasonable steps to avoid it. The Extreme Maverick isn't interested if the other person is hurt. The end justifies the means, so long as he gets his own way, 'everything's good!'

Extreme Mavericks suffer little guilt and almost no conscience. If the other person is hurting, this can be rationalised and justified so that in most situations, the Extreme Maverick has little cognitive dissonance. A Socialised Maverick, can however, internally absorb causing someone pain and they will feel bad about it, wondering if they should have done something different. They will consider this question, at least for a little while, before justification sets in. They can, if desired, reduce any cognitive dissonance to dissipate any bad feelings they are having.

The Socialised Maverick will experience guilt or a twang of conscious but can usually work through it by dint of their analytical and practical nature. A Socialised Maverick is a pragmatist at heart.

The maverick journey never truly ends, although it can plateau at times. Therefore, a maverick can be thought of as a wolf brought into the house to be domesticated, like a dog. Whilst it may become more socialised it will always remain an animal that may turn wild at any moment. With enough pressure (internal or external) the extreme side of the Socialised Maverick will resurface, surprising many. Perhaps the best way to describe the temperament of a Socialised Maverick is one of a sleeping volcano or a domesticated wolf.

Mavericks can be male or Alpha female, Socialised or Extreme, introverted or extraverted. Many flavours of the same drink, although none will 'taste' the same!

An introvert is different from being a shy person. Shy people fear social interactions. An introvert is best described as someone who gets their energy from a quiet environment, and being alone. Introverts typically get exhausted and overwhelmed by being around too many people for too long. Whilst they may enjoy being around people they prefer to do this in small doses. Introverts tend to be more reserved than extraverts.

Extraverts are people who get their energy from being around others, who are outgoing and talkative. When extraverts feel overwhelmed or low, they tend to spend time around others rather than in solitary pursuits.

I believe that there are few people who are at the extremes of introversion or extraversion, we all share traits of both. (However, circumstances and environments can dictate behaviour). For example, whilst your personality may presuppose extrovert behaviour you may experience intense introversion at times or vice versa.

Almost everyone can identify an extraverted maverick because they like to be open with their views and have their behaviour known to others. Introverted mavericks are slyer, preferring to work by stealth and appearing unassuming. Like their extraverted counterparts, they can also be Socialised or Extreme in personality. However, it is fair to say that an *introverted maverick is an enigma* and their behaviour is harder to observe and determine.

Whilst extraverted mavericks are easier to spot and understand, it would be a brave person that ignored the introverted maverick. Mavericks present their maverickism differently depending on whether they are introverted or extraverted and they will need different leadership methods to harness their talent for the greater good.

What are the key maverick attributes?

I'm often asked what is it that makes mavericks different from other individuals. The answer is surprisingly complex, covering personality, mindset, and level of maverickism to name a few. However, as a default, I have found that mavericks always use the acronym WHINES to achieve their best results.

It becomes easier to understand maverick attributes when utilising the acronym WHINES:

Wilful intention
Honest belief
Influential
k**N**owledgeable
Execution and output driven
Success driven

W is for wilful intention

One of the things that angers and frustrates others about mavericks is that mavericks appear to do whatever they want, whenever they feel like, with hardly any consequences or thoughts about the consequences that the maverick's actions have on others. Mavericks appear to have a total disregard for the status quo preferring to do the one thing that is guaranteed to upset the apple cart the most.

These assumptions that mavericks just like to cause problems is not strictly true. Once the maverick has examined the current status quo, they often discover that the existing status quo has arisen through laziness (a full review of the options was never undertaken), or without any intellectual rigour to ascertain whether the current status quo is still fit for purpose.

People tend to prefer to make small incremental changes rather than transformational ones, which is frustrating for both the maverick and the non-maverick. Mavericks often make good consultants, because they can steer their way through office politics, without hampering their thinking. They will seek the best solution not the one that will upset people the least or requires little upheaval or time to make the change.

By having wilful intention as a key maverick attribute, you can be assured that the maverick will be focused on solving and implementing the correct solution to the problem, in the most efficient way. To understand the term wilful intention as it relates to the maverick context, we will need to first look at the dictionary definition of the individual words wilful and intention. Wilful suggests a stubborn persistence in doing what one wishes, especially in opposition to those wishes or commands that ought to be respected or obeyed (dictionary.com) Intention is something that you mean to do. Therefore, someone who is determined to do something regardless of what other people think or wish has a *wilful intention.*

Coupled with the execution and outcome driven maverick attribute, the maverick's wilful intention attribute, ensures that he will complete the task that he sets out to achieve. To get an insight into how this might look like, consider Arnold Schwarzenegger's portrayal of the Terminator in the 1984 and 1991 Terminator films. In those two films the Terminator was relentless in his intention to complete his task, refusing to stop until it led to his ultimate destruction and/or salvation. This is analogous with how mavericks with wilful intention approaches a task. The maverick will stop at nothing to achieve their goal. The consequence of this relentless pursuit of their wilful intention could be successful completion, or loss of reputation or perhaps over time, the maverick's job, or key client. The outcome will depend on whether the maverick is Socialised or Extreme.

When considering whether to proceed with their wilful intention, mavericks wouldn't consider not doing something *just* because someone might not like the method or thing that they are proposing to do. The fact that they might upset someone would not be sufficient justification to cease working on their proposal. Even if that person has, on paper, authority over them.

Mavericks believe that no one has authority over them, they alone are in control of their own destiny. Mavericks will, however, comply with others wishes when those wishes make sense or they feel compelled to do so. There is usually a specific reason for this feeling of compulsion and a sense of propriety isn't it!

How mavericks think

Mavericks remain surprised at the haphazard way others appear to conduct themselves. The way that many people appear to start an endeavour without thinking through how it would work or what steps are required for its success seems strange. The idea of a constraint because of someone's feelings is literally thought of as madness or stupidity by the maverick.

Whether it is in the business or personal domain, mavericks prefer to prepare for their activities, to ensure that they achieve the level of success that they will be satisfied with. Mavericks do not like surprises (especially ones where they could end up looking stupid) so they prefer to prepare for all possibilities. This is different from obsessively detailing everything that needs to happen or could go wrong (although some people will do this), it is more akin to considering all outcomes or consequences that might occur. Even more importantly, how the maverick might deal with or respond to the consequences if they do indeed occur.

A maverick always knows what and why they are doing something; keeping the level of unintended consequences to a minimum.

Another outcome of having a wilful intention is that the maverick will achieve their goal regardless of whether they must break rules to do so. This can have both positive or negative consequences; depending on whether the maverick is Socialised or Extreme.

In the workplace, this preference to work around the rules can cause a lot of consternation especially if the organisation is one that loves bureaucracy. It is not unusual for a maverick to decide, for example, to leave their desk on a call centre to walk to another department to resolve a customer complaint personally. This is against the rules as the call centre consultant needs to be glued to their desk to answer incoming calls. The maverick sees a discrepancy between the stated goals of the organisation (putting the customer first) and the experience of the customer (who has spoken to three different people and still hasn't had her complaint resolved).

Whilst the customer is happy that their complaint has finally been resolved and the maverick has a sense of achievement, the manager remains unhappy with the maverick's behaviour. From the manager's perspective, he has an employee who refuses to sit at their desk and answer the phone. This affects his call figures and perhaps his end of year bonus. The manager probably views this as the beginning of his loss of control, fearing that others will follow the maverick and leave their desks seemingly on a whim.

H is for honest belief

Mavericks can be difficult to understand as they don't appear to be motivated by the usual things and seem to have different motivations and drivers from other people. They are also extremely private people despite how gregarious they may seem on the surface. Therefore, it is difficult to predict how they are going to react to something or which things will move them to action, against those that they smile at wryly and choose to do nothing about. Unless the maverick has a deep level of respect for someone it is unlikely that they will share or discuss their motivations.

Mavericks believe that if they share how they think, they become vulnerable to another person. The sharing of the mind is an intimate act not to be shared lightly, in their view. The mere act of sharing gives another individual the tools to manipulate them in the future. Mavericks do not easily give others control of themselves. There needs to be a deep level of trust between you and the maverick before they let their guard down.

Mavericks are a puzzle wrapped up in an enigma and if you go to the trouble of trying to unwrap the puzzle you might just discover a friend for life. At the very least you may discover respect, loyalty, and attention from the maverick. A maverick's attention is an extremely valuable commodity.

All mavericks are motivated by their own honest belief, which is not necessarily an objective assessment of whether the belief is a good one or not. Maverick's internal drivers consume them; and they are compelled in the first instance, to follow those drivers.

Mavericks are not argumentative for the hell of it (although for the uninitiated it may appear so), they are usually argumentative or challenging for a specific identifiable reason. They have a strong sense of *'the truth'* and will pursue *'the truth'* regardless of the consequences of doing so.

Here lies the nub of the challenge between understanding the honest belief of Socialised and Extreme Mavericks. Socialised Mavericks will take great care to ensure that *'the truth'*, is an objective truth, that will stand the test of time. They will seek out as much data as possible to be sure that they are making a good decision. Socialised Mavericks can always answer the question 'Why do you think that?' sensibly and with reasoned argument. Because of this, they are often persuasive and influential, and people are genuinely happy to follow where they lead.

Extreme Mavericks have more trouble answering the question 'Why?' This is because this type of maverick can hold an honest belief based on just their own opinion garnered from sources which may not be credible to most of the objective populace. If the 'facts' that they discover, fits with what the maverick wants to do or believe, then it will be used as evidence to support their view. If they don't they will ignore this inconvenient truth.

The above is an example of where the internal motivation of the maverick can and does work against him. He is likely to take his (distorted) honest belief and link it to his wilful intention and can become an almost unstoppable machine of self-interest. This as you can imagine is rarely for the greater good and can be quite destructive of people, processes, or companies.

Unless you are a trusted, credible resource to the maverick you will be unable to shake him from his opinion or course of action. The presentation of facts from someone who he does not respect will not move him unless it is linked with things he needs and is in a format where he can loudly and publicly save face and pronounce that 'he was right all along but he has chosen to follow a different way (yours)'. It must appear to everyone that he made the decision to change without outside influences. It must look like he has been magnanimous in changing his mind.

Dependent on the issue this may be an ok process to follow (allowing the maverick to appear to be in control). There is, however, an inherent danger in following this approach. The Extreme Maverick may see you as someone he can dominate and you will find that managing him or even leading him will be difficult in the future.

The key then, to understanding why a maverick is doing what they are doing, is to discover what honest belief is driving them. If you are in the midst of their challenging behaviour or in an argument with them; it is imperative to ignore the smoke screen of the discourse and get to the nub of the issue.

For example, the maverick's fear could cloud the honest belief, and therefore the challenging behaviour is a fear response and not an anger one. In this case, tread carefully, and consider the analogy of a trapped animal and do not allow the maverick to feel cornered. If you do you will get an impassioned fight that will be most certainly damaging in its wake, and not only to the people involved.

Perhaps the honest belief is driven by the 'certainty' that existing processes are fundamentally bad or ineffective. Here the desire to improve things drives the behaviour. There is an inherent danger here also. Socialised Mavericks will push for change; they will attempt to influence others to make it happen. They will break the rules to force the process to bend to their will and you will see some impressive results. In an inflexible workplace, this approach will be problematic especially if the organisation is more concerned with the rules being followed than the results.

In an environment like this the Socialised Maverick will eventually opt out emotionally and mentally, finally choosing to leave the organisation. They may mainly cause damage to the organisation through poor morale of others as they influence them through their (the maverick's) time of disillusionment.

An Extreme Maverick is likely to keep pushing for change, using his brute energy to force through his ideas. Of course, if he is working within a bureaucratic organisation this will be seriously problematic. He will try to manipulate others into following his example and even if he is categorically told that the company will not change to accommodate him he will not let the matter drop. He will look for ways to get them to change their minds and will be very loud in the process. Expect to see significant disruption and cliques amongst his peer group forming. Extreme Mavericks subscribe to the view that 'if you are not for me, then you are against me'. Therefore, they will start manipulating others to join their gang and penalising those that don't. This can rapidly lead to a polarised and oppressive working environment.

I is for influential

Without trying all mavericks are influential.

> Sophie was in a bad mood, she was upset with her manager who had just criticised her unfairly whilst increasing her workload, and she had also slept badly due to some personal issues. She didn't want to talk to anyone, so she got up, closed the door, and returned to her chair.
>
> She sighed, fought back tears, and stared back at her computer. It was going to be a long day.
>
> Phillip glanced up and saw Sophie close her office door. He raised his eyebrows in surprise, 'that's unusual' he

thought. Phillip knew that Sophie always kept her door open, she liked to see and hear what was happening in the open plan office and she wanted to ensure that everyone knew that she was approachable and that they could drop by and see her anytime.

He slowly got up, knocked softly, and walked in.

Phillip: Hi! Everything ok? *(He asks cheerfully)*

Sophie: *(Glances up and gives a weak smile)* Can I help you Phillip? *(said in a despondent voice)*

Phillip: Er, no I just wanted to know whether you are ok? *(pulling up a chair and sitting down)*

Sophie: Oh, er, yes. I'm fine *(said quietly)* Just a little busy.

Phillip: Oh *(gets up quickly)*, I'll be going then.

Phillip leaves and returns to his desk, thinking deeply. He was certain that he saw tears in her eyes, something he's never seen before.

He pondered, and concluded that something must be seriously wrong. Perhaps there were going to be redundancies in the company and she couldn't tell him about it yet? Hadn't he just seen the Director leave her office? Whilst he was considering this, a member of his staff approached him to ask a question. Phillip distractingly answered him, forgoing the usual pleasantries and banter. His employee concluded that 'Phillip had been told some really bad news by Sophie', as Phillip was very happy before he went to see her. When this employee saw one of his colleagues approach Phillip to talk to him, the employee stopped him.

Employee 1: Hey, I wouldn't see Phillip just now, unless it is urgent *(said in a concerned hushed voice)*

Employee 2: Oh, why? *(lowering his voice with curiosity)*

Employee 1: I don't know, but he just got some really bad news from Sophie and he doesn't want to talk about it

Both employees spend ten minutes discussing what this bad news could be and what implications it may have for the company. At the end of their conversation they both repeat and embellish their conversation to their friends in other departments.

This pattern is repeated for the rest of the next hour. Six more managers enter Sophie's office to discuss an issue, and return confused and concerned about her distraction and lack of banter. She is downcast and unhappy and is acting unusually. She finds it difficult to look them in their eye.

Each manager leaves more unhappy and despondent than when they arrive. They are quiet with their employees, and very reflective. The employees gather together to discuss and conclude that their manager has received some bad news from Sophie and is unable to tell them yet. Perhaps the rumour of redundancies is true after all?

After an hour, Sophie stretches at her desk. What a morning, she reflected. She's had 7 managers in her office wanting to talk and all she wanted to do was curl up, lick her wounds, and concentrate on the next thing. Sophie had found it so hard to look them in the eye, because she was sure she would cry and 'spill the beans' on why she was so unhappy. The Director's unfairness and criticisms had pushed her over the edge this morning. She realised that she hated him and now wanted to leave.

If only she could tell this to at least one of her friends that had come to see her this morning, perhaps she would be feeling better by now?

Sophie, sighed and stood up. 'You know', she thought, 'I'm going to go and see them now and see what they really wanted earlier. Just talking about something else will help cheer me up and distract me'.

She opened her door and left her office, noting the worried look Phillip gave her. 'I must see how he is when I get back, I wonder what's the matter with him?' she thought. Sophie took a long walk around the offices to get to each manager. She was surprised about how hushed the offices were and how despondent the employees looked. 'Why is everyone so miserable?', she pondered.

Unfortunately, she couldn't see any of the managers as they were now in meetings so she grabbed Phillip on the return to her office.

Sophie: Have you got a minute?

Phillip: *(He notices the looks his staff give him, as he enters her office, and shuts the door)* Yes?

Sophie: What's going on? Why is everyone in the company so glum?

Phillip: It's because of the redundancies, everyone knows about them but no-ones been told any detail.

Sophie: Redundancies?

Phillip and Sophie have a brief discussion and Sophie (who is a Socialised Maverick and therefore very self-aware) realises that it's her odd behaviour that started the rumour. They have never seen her so concerned and non-communitive and had incorrectly concluded that this reaction was because something bad was going to happen to them.

She realised that by trying to appear professional and saying nothing about her concerns had started a panic. Sophie could have been a little vulnerable with Phillip, who was someone she trusted within the organisation, and told him a little about what was going on with her. She sighed.

Sophie: There are no redundancies. I've just got a few things on my plate right now. Personal issues that I don't want to talk about and the Director chewed me out over something that wasn't my fault and it just added to my worries. Sorry, I wasn't available to you before. *(She smiles at him)*

Phillip: *(pulls up a chair and sits down).* Is that all? You know you can talk to me about whatever? *(He smiles back)*

Sophie: Yeah, I know, thanks

They spend a few minutes discussing what Phillip originally came to discuss. When he finishes, he exits the office leaving Sophie's door open. His employee that came to see him before, asks him whether everything is all right, indicating Sophie.

Phillip: Yeah, why shouldn't it be? *(smiling)*

Employee 1: Er, no redundancies then?

Phillip: No redundancies

Employee 1: What's up with Sophie then?

Phillip: Nothing for you to worry about, it's personal. Cut her some slack and get back to work! *(they both grin at each other and Phillip* *notices that the first thing his employee does on return to his desk, is reach for the phone. Phillip smiles and gets back to work himself).*

About an hour later, Sophie leaves her desk searching out the managers to see if they still needed her. She notes with satisfaction the differences between her earlier visit and now. There is an industrial buzz in the offices and the employees seem happy and engaged.

Later she pondered on what had happened. Is it possible that her mood really affected 300 people that quickly? Why did that happened and how did she unknowingly influence them?

Mavericks are natural influencers and people tend to look to them for cues as to what to think or how to behave. Therefore, if they are acting unusually, or there is a surprising change in their character, then a lot of energy will be expended to discover or ponder why. It's a survival instinct, they know that an unhappy maverick can cause a lot of disruption to the company or the people in it. How much will be dependent on the type of maverick and their maturity levels. This concern (for the maverick's happiness), when it's a Socialised Maverick acting out of character, quickly morphs into fear if it's an Extreme Maverick acting differently. This is because Socialised Mavericks do their best not to harm others. Extreme Mavericks have no compunction in punishing others for displeasing them.

Mavericks need to be aware that just by being themselves, without any intention or forethought, they will influence others. Whether they are unusually exuberant or sad! This can be a terrible burden at times and most Socialised Mavericks will tire of the unspoken responsibility at some point and will need to find an activity that they can truly relax into, before they pick up the yoke again. This ability to unintentionally influence, will never seem like a burden to the Extreme Maverick, as he doesn't care about the consequences of his actions or non-action. Every man for himself is his motto.

N is for kNowledgeable

It is an obvious fact that your ability to influence others is hindered if you are not knowledgeable in your chosen field. Another essential fact is that without exception, all mavericks are concerned with getting their own way (regardless of how open or covert they are with this intention), so they are always considering what tools they need, to become more influential than they already are.

> David was 17 years old and had just begun his first real job in an insurance company. He had been hired as an administrator (a job that he found enjoyable although pathetically easy and not at all intellectually stimulating); even though he knew he would tire of the job within a few months. There was a lot of potential within the company and the career path was a good one. David knew that he was not prepared to wait years to have a position of authority or influence in the company, so he considered his options.

Firstly, he considered the Section Managers in the department. He contemplated their various strengths and weaknesses.

Some of the things that he considered were as follows:

- Which managers were good at their jobs, and respected in them?
  Which specialisms were they good at?
- Which were helpful and willing to teach him the ropes?
- Which employees were likely to get jealous or obstructive as his knowledge grew?
- Whether his Section Manager would get upset (and if so, how to handle this), when he sought other people's advice or knowledge.

David then considered his administrator role. What was its function and dependencies? Which people, or departments, were affected by his work output? What was the composition of the role?

By deliberating on his role, David realised that there was an aspect of the role that had an unmovable 2 week task that the whole office depended on. This task happened mid-month every month. The other 2 weeks were spent completing his other tasks.

David was blessed with three things. The first was that his Department Manager was a Socialised Maverick, who was prepared to ignore convention and allow David to step outside his role and move into or learn other areas as an exercise of potential opportunities and perhaps future successes. The Socialised Maverick manager took a calculated risk on him.

The previous incumbent of the role was considered very good in her job, but David could see that she was inefficient. She dragged out many aspects of the role so that she could work at an extremely leisurely pace. The third thing about the role was that the tasks were not an intellectual challenge for him. It would not take him long before he was considered extremely knowledgeable.

By his third month, David knew all aspects of his role and could be relied on to complete it accurately. David then moved towards making it 'lean'. He removed any processes that were no longer necessary or were long winded, reducing them only to essential parts. He mapped the tasks' dependencies and where possible moved them around in the month to make the task more efficient. (For example, during his mid-month task he was very busy and the other 2 weeks he had hardly anything to do. He moved some of the non-essential tasks from mid-month to other times in the month).

David also got to know the people in the other departments who had an impact on his role. He became friends with them and learned how their jobs worked and how he could make it easier for them. He nurtured and developed strong networks across the office, understanding that these networks would become essential as his own career progressed.

By month four David was deliberately completing his administrator role early leaving him with lots of empty days to fill. He approached Marcus, one of the other

Section Managers that he had identified as good at and respected in their role. Marcus was keen and friendly and David asked Marcus to teach him, Marcus' own role. (David avoided his own Section Manager, who wanted to fill David's day with filing and photocopying).

David's attentions flattered Marcus and he readily agreed to teach him how to underwrite. Soon David was learning the different aspects of underwriting and needed very little supervision. David approached his contacts in the Claims department and began learning how to process and decide a claim. He realised that if you knew the things that a claim handler considered when deciding a claim, then it would make you a better underwriter. He was surprised that no one had exploited this obvious connection before.

David did two more things. He began studying for the Insurance exams so that he could gain some academic knowledge, and he developed close links with the Insurance Agents and Claims Handlers that worked directly with the customer. He developed a good understanding of their roles and the impact that it had on the office staff. David continued to work with different Section Managers to learn different aspects and specialisms of the role. He continued to complete his administrator role diligently and efficiently.

In a relatively short time David moved from being a very knowledgeable underwriter to an expert in underwriting. By the time, he was 18 he had been given the underwriting authority of a Section Manager and had lost all his administrator responsibilities.

In the above example, David wanted to move away from a basic administrator role into one with more responsibility. He quickly surmised that he needed to rapidly increase his knowledge in an area that was considered (by others), complex and difficult to learn. His age would be against him, as well as the industry's culture. In the insurance culture having Section Manager underwriting authority would normally take at least 5 years to achieve. This knowledge activated his wilful intention, making him determined to achieve the influence and authority he desired. David perceived that this would give him the challenge that he needed to truly enjoy his job and stay with the company.

David was not just knowledgeable in his subject area he was also aware of the experience and touch points that he needed to know and experience to be better at his job.

Therefore, being extremely knowledgeable was an essential first step to success. Mavericks are usually uncannily knowledgeable in their area of expertise, and therefore speak with authority on the subject. When they state an opinion based on this knowledge they are rarely wrong, and the method that they use to articulate their knowledge is often interpreted as arrogant behaviour (especially if the maverick is still learning how to become a Socialised Maverick). This misinterpretation can lead to the maverick feeling frustrated or angry; which has its own consequences.

Mavericks need to be intellectually challenged (or they will, over time, literally feel that they are dying), so will naturally seek to improve their knowledge in an area of interest. It is also fair to say that mavericks have an almost pathological issue with being considered stupid. (In fact, Extreme Mavericks will 'go to war' if they even suspect that you consider them stupid.

E is for execution and output driven

One of the biggest failings of managers is that they are often not execution and output driven. They may be able to 'talk a good game', in such that they have many good cogent ideas on what needs to be achieved, or the effect that a change may have on a situation, but when pushed, they appear clueless on exactly how this change should be achieved. They have planned the communication and implementation of the change but not whether the change will have the desired effect. They are in fact wishing that if the implementation goes well, a good outcome will naturally fall out from it.

> Joanne worked for a company that had decided that rather than having a few functional departments staffed with highly experienced (and expensive) staff they could reduce the number of staff in these departments, by transitioning into a call centre model. Some of these expensive staff could move to the call centre and become generalists rather than specialists. As these highly expensive specialists left (the good specialists would get bored and would prefer to keep their skills sharp and work for a company that valued their specialism), they could be replaced with cheap generalists. These generalists would not be expected to know the detail of everything, they would pass the details (but not the call) to the functional departments for later completion; if they were unable to help the customer during the call. The company would also have the benefit of having many calls concentrated into one place, with more (and cheaper), people completing the calls.
>
> On the surface, this appeared to be an excellent idea, although Joanne who was a highly trained,

knowledgeable, and experienced specialist could see the flaws.

One day the manager of the call centre had an excellent idea. The specialists on the call centre were complaining about the quality of work now undertaken by the company since the call centre model had been implemented. They could tell by the detail of customer complaints, when the customers called the call centre, that the company's standards had fallen and that the customer was right to complain. The functional departments had become lazy, they were doing shoddy work, if any at all, because they knew that the call centre staff would eventually pick up and correct any errors that they made. Or ideally complete the work in the first place.

The call centre was in the middle of an open plan office and could see the other departments working at their desks. What they saw was galling, their non call centre colleagues were spending a vast amount of time, walking around, laughing, and clearly not working hard. Meanwhile the call centre was inundated with work. It was easier for the call centre to just complete the work as it came in on a call, rather than complete a 'Yellow peril' (this was a handwritten request from the call centre for the department to complete a customer action. It was completed on yellow paper so it would stand out when it reached the department and be treated as urgent); requesting the correct department to fulfil the work. Once a 'Yellow peril' was sent, the call centre staff had to update the computer system so that everyone could see what needed to be done.

This was very time consuming and not at all effective as the same member of staff would receive a phone call a week later, complaining that the action had not been taken or had been completed incorrectly.

The manager of the call centre's excellent idea was that every time the call centre found an error, it was to be recorded by the call centre staff onto a 'White peril'. The 'White peril' was then sent to the relevant department and the call centre staff member would record the department that made the mistake on a running tally.

At first Joanne thought this was a great idea, it meant that over time the high volume of calls would reduce, the departments would be responsible for their errors and the call centre could return to their stated purpose. Their purpose was to be the hub of customer contact, completing simple non-technical actions and advice to the customer.

The functional specialists would complete any complicated or detailed advice instead of the call centre staff. The call centre staff had ridiculous call targets. Each call was not to exceed 3 minutes which was impossible if each member had to correct unnecessary errors.

In the first two weeks, hundreds of 'White perils' had been completed and the call centre staff were looking forward to a reduced workload. Then a curious thing happened. The 'White perils' that each member of staff had completed was returned to them. They had the word SEEN written at the top in capitals.

Joanne asked her manager 'what did this mean?' He explained that the functional departments had complained that there were too many errors ('White perils'), and they were unable to accept the increased workload (remember these were the mistakes that the functional departments had made), so they were acknowledging that they had seen the error, but it needed to be fixed by the call centre staff (in between calls, thus eliminating any down time that they had; which was extremely small if at all, most days).

Joanne surmised that the new process was now:

- Answer the call (listen to the customer fume about an error).
- Not give the customer any relief in that moment, just platitudes.
- Record in detail the error on a 'White peril'.
- Record in detail the error on the computer system.
- Record error on your personal tally system.
- Speak to the angry customer at least twice more when they complain that nothing has changed.
- Watch the workload on the call centre go up as it takes longer to complete each call.
- Watch your call statistics plummet and risk disciplinary action for not 'working efficiently enough'.
- Wait two weeks for the 'White peril' to return to you so that you can correct the original error.
- Watch nothing change in terms of customer satisfaction and work efficiency.

This was complete madness and Joanne couldn't understand why her manager was unable to see that the above process did nothing to improve the quality of the work nor reduce the workload of his staff.

It wasn't long before Joanne and her persuaded colleagues, implemented a new unofficial process.

- Answer the call (listen to the customer fume about an error)
- Fix the error yourself
- Update the computer system
- Do not complete any other paperwork

Within days of this unofficial process being implemented, the Call Centre Manager was celebrating the improved quality of work undertaken, measured, of course, by the now non-existent completed 'White perils'. No 'White perils' no quality issues.

Yes, really!

This lack of insight is one of the things that inflames mavericks the most. In the above example the manager believed he was instrumental in improving quality. He had completely failed to assess the outcome of his change and only managed to decrease morale in his department and lose all credibility and respect, making it harder for any future proposals to receive support.

It is usually when it is clear to the maverick that the manager is not execution and output driven, that these managers believe that the maverick is deliberately hindering the manager's ability to affect change. Mavericks will test their own hypothesis (that the change will in fact, not achieve the stated aim) by asking lots of questions. Of course, their favourite question is why! Sometimes channelling the persistent toddler, or a dog with a bone!

Mavericks are not interested in other people's egos and will not 'move into action' if it's obvious to them that action will not fundamentally change the status quo to an acceptable (to them) level. Mavericks believe in getting things done; they are completely perplexed and annoyed with people that spend a lot of time talking about something without the intention of executing the action. Equally annoying is people that start a task and then let it fizzle out without completion.

All mavericks agree with Stephen Covey's 2nd Habit from his book, 7 Habits of Highly Effective People. This Habit states that you should 'begin with the end in mind'. It refers to the need to begin with a clear vision of your desired output then planning backwards to achieve it. This ties in with the maverick's execution and output driven attribute and is therefore readily adopted by them.

S is for success driven

Mavericks usually do not see the point of doing something that will end in failure, a consequence of their execution and output driven maverick attribute working within them. This is the reason Joanne in the above example, stopped following her manager's quality initiative, and persuaded others to do so as well.

This refusal to commit to an action destined to fail is one of the reasons that there can be friction in the workplace with mavericks and their managers. Socialised and Extreme Mavericks will argue against implementation of a task that will fail or hasn't gone through a rigorous assessment for success and will work hard to influence or manipulate others away from the proposed change. If the manager is not respected or even credible, he will have a hard job persuading the maverick to be an active and willing catalyst for change. Dependent on the maverick he may have to work hard to maintain authority or credibility in his position of manager and/or leader as well.

Mavericks have little tolerance for doing something where failure can be foreseen without the potential of using that failure to lead to success later. This is because, whilst all mavericks, are primarily motivated by the execution and output driven maverick attribute; the success driven maverick attribute is a motivating close second.

Most mavericks cannot see the point of doing something that they are unlikely to be a success in. After all, they expect and enjoy being judged as competent and successful in their endeavours. Mavericks also love challenge, risk and being pulled out of their comfort zone. They do not mind failing, if that failure enables them to understand how to be successful in their endeavours in the future. Failure is often embraced as much as success is.

When reading the above, there seems to be some dichotomy in the insistence that mavericks will only do something that they can be successful in and the statement that mavericks have no fear of failing! This confusion is resolved when you consider that mavericks are intrinsically motivated and value their own opinion (along with a very few select individuals) over others. They are just not interested in the 'everyone does it this way' school of thinking.

Mavericks will therefore establish the parameters of the success criteria for the endeavour they are undertaking, before they begin. Prior to beginning, for example, the maverick can decide beforehand that it is ok to fail at a task because failure has excellent learning potential. Thus, if the maverick has determined that failure is ok, and they do fail, that failure meets their success criteria. (Many scientists subscribe to this world view, and most mavericks see life as a series of experiments with hypothesis that need to be explored and proven).

Mavericks excel in the pursuit of success whilst embracing the possibility of failure.

It is worth noting, however, that it is the maverick's definition of success that he will pay attention to, not yours. Thomas Edison (prolific inventor), was an excellent example of someone who demonstrated, at the very least, maverick behaviours in his endeavours.

Whilst inventing the lightbulb he is quoted as saying: 'I have not failed. I've just found 10,000 ways that won't work'. Another favourite quotation of his, which could just be the mantra of every maverick out there, is the following: 'Hell, there are no rules here – we're trying to accomplish something'.

Being successful (however the maverick defines that success) is important to the maverick in two ways. Firstly, there is internal satisfaction, being successful bolsters the maverick's self-esteem and confidence levels. Secondly, success is needed for the maverick to influence or manipulate others into fulfilling the maverick's intentions in the manner that the maverick is expecting. It is essential therefore, that the maverick has a history of success; or can detail how their venture will become successful in time.

The world loves a winner and people will tend to follow someone who can guarantee them success, or provide them with a pathway to success.

Mavericks recognise that having 'natural' leadership ability (maverick attributes) is essential in the art of influence. In fact, John C Maxwell (leadership author, speaker, and Pastor), states that 'leadership is influence nothing more, nothing less'. I agree that leadership has a strong influence component.

For a maverick, if you cannot influence, you *have* nothing, you *are* nothing. Influence is a core need and driver for the maverick. If they cannot influence, task or people, the maverick will work hard to find a way to attain some level of influence. Dependent on whether the maverick is Socialised or Extreme will determine whether this will be a relative painful experience or not, for the company or authority in charge.

If influence is not forthcoming Socialised Mavericks will eventually leave, taking a lot of knowledge and capability with them. Extreme Mavericks may also leave but not before they have caused a lot of disruption and destruction behind them.

Leadership is everything, and only a fool truly believes that leadership is a job title or something that the aspiring individual has no control over. For true influence to take place there needs to be character and competence.

Socialised Mavericks inherently understand this and work hard to become true leaders. Unlike many individuals, they will not focus solely on improving their competence. All mavericks recognise, however, that being highly competent is the first stage to ensuring that you have expert influence.

When you have, expert influence you can influence people and tasks based on areas of your expertise. You are sought out for your knowledge and input, becoming the 'go to' specialist. The maverick can wield a lot of authority in a narrow area, which can provide significant influence.

Expert influence can provide enough challenge for both the Socialised and Extreme Maverick. Most extraverted Socialised Mavericks yearn for more influence (not necessarily position authority) however, and will continue working on their character. They will do the necessary self-work to become someone who is, and can be trusted and someone who is and can demonstrate a high level of integrity.

Extreme Mavericks are less concerned about their character as an important component for their ability to lead. After all, they are more concerned about their ability to manipulate others and have no compunction against using brute force. They will work extremely hard in becoming the acknowledged expert and often work in positions where their success depends on their expertise.

In terms of character Socialised Mavericks will work hard on becoming trusted. Trust comes in two forms, the ability to be trusted and the ability to be trustworthy. It is possible to trust someone who is not trustworthy. Therefore, Extreme Mavericks still benefit from people who trust them.

Trustworthiness relates to character and being trusted could include character traits but also focuses on credibility. This credibility is the area of trust that Extreme Mavericks will work on.

They know that the marriage of competence and credibility will lead to expert leadership. They will work on increasing their credibility with others. Expert leadership and their own force of nature will enable them to manipulate others to do their bidding. For most Extreme Mavericks, this is enough.

2. The Maverick Mindset

"Manipulators rarely advise you to seek new and diverse information or to learn and research for yourself, it tends to be safer for exploitative and irresponsible leaders to keep their citizens in the dark; in their view, less independent thought is the better. Independent thought leads to an inquiring mind, a mindset that eventually leads to the questioning of authority figures, and that is the one thing that inadequate leaders do not want"

– Teresa Stover

In any discussion on mavericks, it is important to acknowledge that there is a difference between those who have a maverick personality and those that have maverick traits. To truly understand the maverick mindset there is a need to separate these two concepts.

The Big 5 Personality traits

The study of 'personality' has kept psychologists busy for several years, and there are numerous differing theories and concepts on the subject. The most popular theory right now is the 'Big 5 Personality traits'. This theory proposes that there are 5 broad dimensions to personality. They are (Wikipedia 2016):

1. **Openness to experience** (inventive/curious vs consistent/cautious)

2. **Conscientiousness** (efficient/organised vs easy going/careless)

3. **Extraversion** (outgoing/energetic vs solitary/reserved)

4. **Agreeableness** (friendly/compassionate vs analytical/detached)

5. **Emotional Stability** (secure/confident vs sensitive/nervous)

If there are no strong preferences in all of the five dimensions, then an individual's personality can be viewed in one of two ways:

1. Adaptable, moderate, reasonable
2. Unprincipled, inscrutable, calculating

Considering this definition, individuals who do not have strong preferences cannot be classified as a maverick nor are they demonstrating maverick behaviour. It is a common misconception to assume that someone who is unprincipled, inscrutable and calculating is a maverick. Mavericks are always highly principled even if, in the case of Extreme Mavericks, the principles that they uphold are base, immoral, or unethical.

If we use the Big 5 Personality Trait Theory as a basis for considering maverick personality, we can see that mavericks tend to score highly in the 'Openness to experience' trait. This usually demonstrates that mavericks are likely to be more creative, curious, and aware of their feelings than other people. They are more likely to hold unconventional beliefs or ideas and prefer novelty over routine. Mavericks hate any routine determined by others with a passion and are always searching for new challenges. If unchallenged at work, a Socialised

Maverick will disengage with the organisation, withdraw their effort, and look for challenges elsewhere. Their reduced effort will not be immediately noticeable as their work output will be on par with the rest of their work colleagues. Over time, however, the company will notice the reduction of the maverick's usual output and enthusiasm. Eventually the unchallenged and bored Socialised Maverick will leave the organisation.

> Jane was fed up, whilst she didn't mind working harder than everyone else (she enjoyed her work), it was, however, becoming annoying. It was obvious that she was 'carrying' several employees. These employees came in late and did inferior work.
>
> Whilst she gave the company her 'everything', her colleagues appeared in contrast to have an easy time. The manager of the department had become to rely on Jane's input and was therefore increasing his demands on her. Jane had even taken to coming into the office a couple of hours early (around 7 am when no one was in), to get more work done.
>
> Once her boss had worked out that she was regularly in the office early, he would call her before he left home or on his way into work, (between 7-8.30am) to give her additional work. He also encouraged other employees to call her to record their absence (instead of speaking to their own manager when the Office was officially open). This soon negated the advantage of Jane coming in early, as she was unable to do her own work, effectively becoming the company answer machine during those early hours. This was far outside the scope of her job, and a source of great frustration.

Jane's additional effort although never acknowledged or appreciated, soon became something to be expected. Jane as a Socialised Maverick knew that she had to do something about the situation before she lost her temper and did something that she would later regret. She could feel herself being pulled to behave as an Extreme Maverick and was sure that if she did, one of the resulting consequences would be the loss of her job.

Jane was experiencing significant cognitive dissonance, so decided to reduce her output, and adjust her hours to her contractual ones. She would then be able to accept the fact that her colleagues were not pulling their weight as she was no longer picking up the slack; or being taken advantage of.

After a while it became obvious to her boss that something in the department had changed. Not only had Jane's attitude to her work appeared to be different, it was clear that she had become increasingly insular. (Jane was looking for new jobs and attending interviews. She was also finding it increasingly difficult working with her colleagues whom she believed was not pulling their weight and taking advantage of her own work ethic. Jane decided that it was no longer justifiable for her to work harder than them). When her boss asked her to stay late or come in early to pick up the slack from an inefficient colleague, she politely refused each 'invitation'.

Eventually, her boss was at a complete loss and becoming increasingly desperate; his manager was asking why the department was no longer meeting its deadlines or working as efficiently as it had been previously. He knew it was because Jane was no longer picking up the slack from others and was working within her job description. He eventually called her into his office.

Boss: Hi Jane, is everything ok?

Jane: Yes *(Jane wondered whether he would finally realise that she was no longer working as hard as she was previously, and that he was to blame)*

Boss: You don't seem to be working as hard as you once were. You no longer come in early or help your colleagues out when they don't finish a job

Jane: *(silence)*

Boss: Why is that?

Jane: *(shrugs).* I do my job and I work my hours. Is there a problem with my work? *(Jane had a slightly insolent tone. She wanted a confrontation so she could express what was bothering her)*

Boss: No, your work is good as always, in fact you're my best employee. I can't fault you; your work output is better than anyone that I have. Even now, when you are doing less hours!

Jane: So …

Boss: *(sighs)* it's just that you aren't working as hard as you used to. I need things back the way they were. I appreciated your hard work. I genuinely did. I know I can't tell you off as your work is good, the best even, but it's just frustrating that you could work harder, you just choose not to…

Jane: *(Jane couldn't believe that he didn't take the opportunity to have a real discussion. If he had done so, then things could have changed but she didn't intend to make the conversation any easier for him. He didn't respect her, and she had lost respect for him. Jane looked at him dispassionately and shrugs)*

An opportunity lost.

Jane did not feel the need to describe how she felt or the reason for her change of attitude. In her eyes, it was obvious why her attitude to her work had changed and her boss had plenty of time to make things right. He should have led the team better. He should have had more courage to tell her what he was *really* thinking and to find out what was the cause for her change in work behaviour. Jane had worked for him for years so he should know her well enough to recognise the red flag that she was putting up. She was disgusted with him and realised sadly that she had lost a great deal of respect for him, and as such was no longer able to work for him.

Jane knew that her boss might offer her a pay rise to stay but she didn't want one. She knew that she would find it extremely difficult to continue working for someone that she did not find credible, someone that she had also lost respect for. Jane had already made the decision to leave, which she did just 4 weeks later. (People that are highly talented in their job, rarely have difficulty finding somewhere to work or managers that will appreciate the unique talents and insight that they bring).

Her department never fully recovered from her departure. It wasn't just the downward adjustment to the work rate; she was the social glue that kept the department running. She could easily link with other departments across the company, because cross departmental working and networking made sense to her and she was good at it. The result of her efforts in this area and her ability to make connections that others couldn't see, meant that it was easier for her department to complete its work quicker and more completely. The department found that it was easy to seek co-operation with employees who worked in different departments because Jane had built solid relationships with influencers in other parts of the company.

The company misunderstood Jane's ability, work rate and ethic. The company knew that the job was being done well, but they didn't know what effort was being put in to make it look like the performance of the job role was as effortless as the job holder had made it seem.

Jane leaving the company was painful but it had the advantage of not being directly damaging. This is not often the case with Extreme Mavericks, especially when they are upset, feeling humiliated or frustrated.

It is likely that if an Extreme Maverick is unchallenged the maverick will start to unravel things to cause some excitement for themselves. This unravelling could be a colleague's emotional state as the maverick manipulates them into doing things that the maverick wants; or the maverick could break something at work, so that they can fix it. This enables them to do something interesting and challenging for a while. It is common for a maverick to set in motion a cycle of fixing and breaking work processes (or people) for want of something to do. (It can take quite a long time, if ever, for the organisation to work out exactly what is going on, especially if the broken work practices are initiated by an introverted maverick).

However, the maverick's love of adventure, abstract and intellect can lead to a surprising complex and challenging maverick nature. This specific trait of the maverick is one of the things often admired and loved by non–mavericks (conformists).

The personality trait 'Conscientiousness' in this context relates to the tendency to strive for achievement, to be self-disciplined, organised and determined. It is worth noting that the maverick will always measure himself against his own measures and standards and no one else's. They are internally motivated and as such generally have little concern for what others think, unless confronted by someone that they respect. This is usually either a fellow maverick, an intellectually superior person or someone highly credible or respected in their subject matter.

(Mavericks will, however, move into action if someone's perceptions are affecting something, or someone, they care about. For example, the wrong perception could be effecting the maverick's reputation and their ability to earn).

Be aware however, to anger the maverick is to awaken the beast!

Unless you are credible in at least one of the above areas you will have little hope of getting the maverick to change their opinion or method of work. Mere rank or hierarchy will not influence the maverick to change. You need a compelling reason for that.

All maverick personalities are highly determined to get their own way, with only the method of achievement differentiating Socialised and Extreme Mavericks. Whilst Socialised Mavericks will consider other's feelings, wants and desires and do their best to accommodate them whilst ensuring that the mavericks goals are met (rarely at the maverick's expense); Extreme Mavericks will focus solely on achieving that goal at the expense of others if necessary.

Most people associate maverickism with those that are highly extraverted. This is a fallacy as a significant number of mavericks are introverted and thus are not as noticeable (to conformists) as their extraverted counterparts. In fact, more 'damage' has occurred by upset introverted mavericks than extraverted ones, it's just not always apparent at first glance!

There is one important deviation from the usual behaviour of introverts when compared to introverted mavericks. Introverts generally prefer not to take the lead in situations, as they would prefer not to have the spotlight on them, which is not true of an introverted maverick. The introverted maverick will happily take the lead in areas that they care about, being decisive, authoritative and controlling; to ensure that things proceed in the way that they feel that they should. In my opinion, introverted mavericks are mavericks that operate in stealth mode.

I think that the biggest variable between Socialised Mavericks and Extreme Mavericks is how 'Agreeable' they are. Socialised Mavericks will value getting along with others and cooperating rather than competing, as compared to Extreme Mavericks (but never as high as a Conformist). Socialised Mavericks are highly competitive, but will hide this competitive streak if it means that it makes it easier for others to cooperate with them and be more easily influenced. One of the peculiarities of the British people is that they do not like to see and is indeed suspicious of overt competitiveness. British Socialised Mavericks have therefore learnt to adapt and often hide their competitive nature to increase their level of success and influence.

Socialised Mavericks will have more empathy towards people, even those not in their social or friendship groups than Extreme Mavericks. Extreme Mavericks will always place their own self-interest at a premium to others and are not shy in showing or expressing this. They have little concern for social harmony unless it fits neatly into their plans. They tend to be more sceptical of others and are therefore likely to be more uncooperative.

Mavericks tend to have high 'Emotional Stability', which in this context means that they tend to be calm in tense situations and rarely lose confidence in their own ability or control of the situation. Mavericks tend to be carefree and optimistic and have a high tolerance for stress. This self-confidence and high self-esteem is often seen as intimidating or arrogant by others, leading to the maverick once again being misunderstood, and immensely frustrated.

An Extreme (extraverted) Maverick may however, demonstrate behaviour that looks like they are unable to control high emotion like anger. This however, is often a ruse employed by them to manipulate other's behaviours. An explosion of anger from an Extreme (extraverted) Maverick is hardly ever truly spontaneous, more likely part of a plan to change someone else's mindset or behaviour. An Extreme Maverick often sees intimidation and domination as an effective tool to get what they want.

E Joyce and A Timothy found in 2004 a correlation between the Big 5 Personality Traits and transformational leadership. It seems that the Socialised Maverick's personality, lends itself directly to someone who is likely to practice transformational leadership. This type of leadership can inspire positive changes for their followers, as the Socialised Maverick focuses on helping every member of the group succeed and develop. Socialised Mavericks always work for the greater good, if it isn't possible in the environment that they find themselves in, they leave.

Below is a summary of the maverick personality in chart form:

The Maverick Personality		
Personality Trait	Extreme Maverick	Socialised Maverick
Openness to experience	Inventive/Curious	Inventive/Curious
Conscientiousness	Efficient/Organised	Efficient/Organised
Extraversion	Extrovert	Extrovert or Introvert
Agreeableness	High analytical/detached (competitive)	Moderate analytical/detached (co-operative)
Emotional Stability	Secure/Confident	Secure/Confident

© The Maverick Personality Chart – Judith Germain 2016

When considering a maverick's personality, aside from deciding whether they are introverts or extroverts, it's worth determining whether they are demonstrating a maverick personality or maverick traits.

The Maverick Continuum™

All individuals are on a © Maverick Continuum Journey™ (see the diagram below), which is a journey of maverickism that is not (and cannot) be fully completed by any individual.

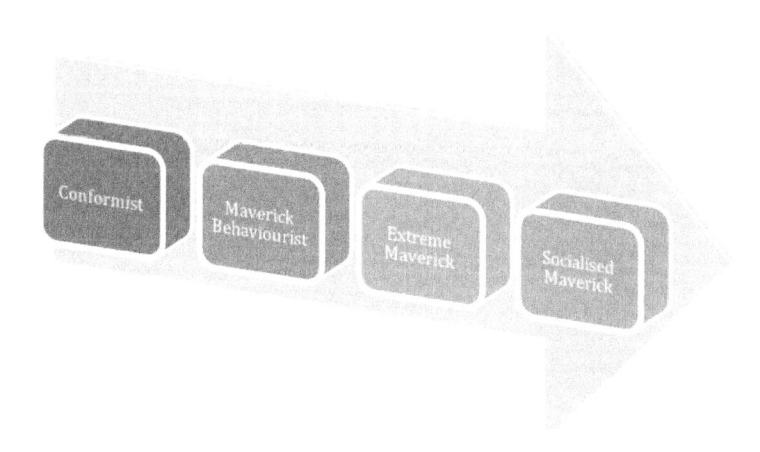

© The Maverick Continuum Journey™[2], Judith Germain 2016

The true Conformist usually, has no desire (unless there is a compelling reason) to demonstrate the depth of determination or risk taking behaviour required to progress in their maverick

---
[2] © The Maverick Continuum Journey™ – Judith Germain 2016

behaviour. They tend to admire the maverick and their results and resent the behaviour as and when it deviates from the norm.

Especially if the altered behaviour affects them.

The Conformist individual can easily be manipulated or influenced by the maverick, especially if they are overly keen to work within agreed rule boundaries and team cultures.

Those that express maverick tendencies, but not personality, will end their maverick journey at the point of Maverick Behaviourist, and will be unable to progress further. This is because the individual is generally a conformist by personality who demonstrates maverick traits, in certain situations. This demonstration is usually in one area of their life.

The most common expression of a Maverick Behaviourist, is an individual who is, a conformist in their 'home life', but demonstrates Socialised Maverick behaviour in their work life.

The first two stations on the Maverick Continuum Journey™, Conformist and Maverick Behaviourist, indicate someone on the Maverick Continuum™ who could eventually or is currently demonstrating maverick traits. If the Conformist can demonstrate enough determination and risk taking in what they are doing, they may be able to behave in a maverick way in a limited facet of their lives. This will enhance their ability to be successful in this area.

It may surprise people that the Extreme Maverick is not shown at the end of the Maverick Continuum™. An Extreme Maverick has not completed their personal growth, although it is highly unlikely that they will agree with this assessment! The reality is that it is common for their (emotional) development to be stunted at 'Extreme Maverick', because at this point of the Maverick Continuum™, extreme behaviour *appears* to be bringing several rewards.

Oft times it is only with a great deal of reflection or acknowledgement by someone the maverick respects and finds credible, that the Extreme Maverick realises that there are other, better ways to get what they want.

The Socialised Maverick is where the Extreme Maverick should wish to end up if they want to work at their full potential! The Socialised Maverick retains their behaviour and attitudes in all areas of their life, having learnt how to soften their approach when speaking and dealing with Conformists.

The Socialised Maverick shares the same opinion that the Extreme Maverick has about Conformists. They believe that Conformists are too sensitive and easily upset or offended. The Socialised Maverick acknowledges that it is easier to influence the Conformist if the maverick moderates their behaviour so that the Conformist can feel comfortable. This change in behaviour by the Socialised Maverick is indicative of the move away from manipulating someone (Extreme Maverick behaviour) to influencing someone (Socialised Maverick behaviour). It is an acceptable and rewarding journey, both for the maverick and the people around him.

It is possible for two Socialised Mavericks to work extremely well together, providing the right mix of innovation, risk taking and influence to make a substantial difference to the task in hand. They will typically focus on what needs doing to guarantee the success of the project and will forego the necessity to stroke their egos (which is essential for the

Extreme Maverick) in preference to the timely execution of the task.

Two Extreme Mavericks can work together, especially if the task in question is short lived, although it is likely that they will find it very difficult. It is in their nature to fight for dominance of the task, and the glory of successful performance that it will bring, which could cause a damaging array of fallout.

However, if both mavericks can see that it is extremely beneficial for them to work together (there is significant reward) then for the duration of the mutual benefit they will co-operate and work together. It is likely that there will be very little trust between the two and as soon as it appears that one maverick can achieve dominance or control over the other, this opportunity will be taken, even to the detriment of successful completion of the task.

The Socialised Maverick has learnt that whilst influencing can be a much longer process than manipulation (at least in the beginning) it is infinitely more rewarding. It is more rewarding because by choosing to influence, the maverick is seeking the Conformist's buy in. This makes it more likely that a 'win/win' situation can be obtained. An important consideration is that manipulation only works for a period of time; eventually other people decide to fight against you or to work under protest (therefore not at their best). It is not possible to get the best out of people by manipulation alone in the long term. People generally do not mind being influenced, if the influence is subtle and clearly for the greater good.

The interesting thing about the Socialised Maverick is that whilst (over a period of time) it can become the default behavioural response by the maverick; under pressure the maverick can slide into Extreme Maverick behaviour very easily. This can surprise, even distress, Conformists because it may appear that they have 'awoken' the maverick; and the subsequent behaviour of the maverick seems 'unlike them' or inconsistent.

What Conformists don't realise is that there is often (at the point of conflict) an internal struggle between Socialised and Extreme behaviour within the Socialised Maverick. The inner dialogue of the maverick can be quite intense at this point, if the maverick has been behaving like a Socialised one for some time then it's likely that Socialised behaviour is the one that will win out, eventually. Although the Socialised Maverick will not like it, feeling like they have compromised themselves for the greater good.

However, whilst the above holds true, this is not to assume that a Socialised Maverick will not demonstrate Extreme Maverick behaviour at times of excessive pressure (for the maverick). If so, stand back as the behaviour change will be spectacular, although fortunately, short lived.

We can be confident then, that a maverick is open to new experiences, preferring novel solutions and is a curious soul. They are highly organised and efficient when planning and executing new tasks. It is important to note, however, that this does not mean that they have a neat and tidy desk; this observation refers to their mind and thought processes. Whilst being able to think of the 'big picture', they do not neglect the small details. This can sometimes mean that they ensure obsessively that others implement the small details that they have planned.

Mavericks can be found anywhere on the extraversion scale and will be analytical and detached in their thinking. Only after the thinking process has ended will Socialised Mavericks temper their detachment with compassion and friendliness; for them any important action is a two-step process (detachment from the issue whilst analytically pondering over it, followed by considerations on the best way to implement the action. This is when thoughts about others, and how to influence them occur).

All mavericks are innately secure and confident in their abilities and have high self-esteem. The only exceptions to this are:

1. When the maverick is still maturing (i.e. a young adult), where they may still experience periods of being unsure about themselves or their actions.

2. Following a life changing event where self-esteem and confidence has taken a serious knock, (for a period of time).

So, what are mavericks really like?

Mavericks will, almost pathologically, search for the truth in all situations, at all times. For Socialised Mavericks, this search will, firstly, be for the objective truth. When this search is coupled with their analytical detachment, many are fooled into believing that mavericks are cold and unfeeling.

Words are very important to the maverick who will apply the literal interpretation of what they are told and do not use their words lightly. Arguments can often ensue when the maverick is discussing what the Conformist has said and the Conformist keeps exclaiming 'that's not what I meant!' Further examination shows that the Conformist was sloppy in their word choice and chose a word that did not accurately convey what they meant. The maverick sees this as an unforgivable sin.

This lack of accuracy annoys the maverick immensely.

A Socialised Maverick will tend to 'let this inaccurate word choice go', only after fully explaining why the Conformist was wrong and why the Socialised Maverick was right. This type of maverick will let go their need to be right (sometimes with some difficulty!) in view of gaining influence or cooperation from another. An Extreme Maverick will never let go of their need to be right, even if this mean that there is a loss of harmony or an increase in hostilities between the parties. If it suits their purposes, they will continue to argue with the Conformist; even when they can recognise that the argument is based on poor word choice rather than disagreement with the issue being discussed.

The next search for truth that the Socialised Maverick, (or the first search for truth for the Extreme Maverick) will make, is 'relative truth', (e.g. what truth are others seeing? And more importantly, how does this 'truth' affect me?). A Socialised Maverick asks these questions so that they understand alternative viewpoints. They will use this to persuade, influence and seek cooperation to complete the task or goal that they have in mind. In contrast an Extreme Maverick will use this information to manipulate and dominate the discussion or action that they need completing.

The biggest difference between a Socialised or Extreme Maverick is their moral dimension. Extreme Mavericks rarely, if at all, consider the moral implications, the consequences of their actions simply don't matter to them. The only important thing is that they get what they want. There is a certain lack of conscience with this group of mavericks, who believe firmly in the 'ends justify the means' argument.

The importance of character

All mavericks without exception, demand honesty and integrity from the people that they work with. Socialised Mavericks expect that the individual should have a good character, be trustworthy and can be relied upon. It is important that this person is trustworthy in all things, as alignment with this individual has an impact on the maverick's reputation. Reputation is important to the Socialised Maverick as he uses his reputation to influence others.

My belief is that reputation is the marriage of integrity and capability which is one of the reasons that Socialised Mavericks are proud of their good reputation. They have both components of reputation. They are highly competent in what they do and they have a track record of success. They tend to be respected for their character, as well as their ability.

Socialised Mavericks expect that the person that they are working or aligned with, is loyal to them. It is slightly different for the Extreme Maverick as his morality is more skewed. He is not concerned with whether the people that he aligns himself with have a good character or not, he is however, morbidly concerned with whether they are loyal to him and can be trusted. Extreme Mavericks do not respond well to betrayal (no matter how small or insignificant the betrayal is). He expects his associates to have an 'us against the world' approach, putting his needs first, even above their own.

Therefore, character is very important for all mavericks, after all, relationships are currency for them. The better the relationship, the more influence or manipulation they have available to them.

Socialised Mavericks struggle working for leaders who have poor character and lack integrity. After many years managing, training and working with all types of managers in all types of industries, I see that the most common aspect in these different types of managers (including leaders), is that there is often a real inability to gain trust from the people that they are managing or leading.

Mavericks respect credibility and if their manager is not trustworthy, has little integrity or competence, then it is unlikely that they will pay much attention to them. Whilst Conformist employees are likely to 'put up or shut up', mavericks will make changes to the situation or workplace. Depending on the type of maverick this could have positive or negative connotations.

Extreme problem solving - looking for flaws in the argument

Mavericks love challenge and risk, and will continuously look for these two components like a heat seeking missile! This can be either frustrating or annoying for Conformists, who often misunderstand the intention of the maverick.

To problem solve is innate for the maverick, as they are a lover of all things new. They excel at problem solving and use the opportunity to provide themselves with a mental challenge and as an opportunity to help others. There is also the self-satisfaction of knowing that a) they were right b) they solved something that others couldn't do).

The maverick's problem solving ability stems from the fact that they are naturally analytical and detached in their mental processes. Whilst considering a problem they can be devoid of the emotion of the conundrum and see things more clearly than others might do.

Mavericks are often misunderstood because it is often felt that they delight in proving that someone else is wrong. This is not usually true. The maverick is trying to solve the stated problem and will ask challenging questions to get to the real crux of the matter. They will then outline what the problem is, in excruciating detail to the other person. Dependent on the maverick's own development, the correction of the other person, may or may not be sensitively handled. If not, it is likely that the explanation will be a painful and perhaps humiliating experience for the other person.

Mavericks have an obsessive need for the truth (objective for Socialised Mavericks and relative for Extreme Mavericks), which is why mavericks find it very difficult to leave a problem unsolved. It doesn't matter if the problem is behavioural, abstract, or substantive.

Often the maverick will solve a problem that the management team would have preferred to be ignored. This often occurs when the company has a misalignment of a stated core value or mission statement with the actual implementation of company policy.

> Robert was the HR Manager of a supermarket when he noticed a discrepancy. Harry, who was the Checkout

Manager, had been praised for running a very efficient department. He hardly paid any overtime to his employees which meant that he was easily within his payroll budget. Customers were very happy as there never seemed to be any queues at the checkout. The mystery shopper results were in and there were high scores for the checkout experience.

The Store and Checkout Managers both benefited from good Mystery Shopper scores. Robert recalled the management meeting and the look of pride on the Checkout Manager's face and the look of disgust on his colleagues.

Something didn't feel right. Robert left his desk and decided to walk the shop floor. He saw the following:

- The grocery department had many empty shelves, despite the time of day and the number of employees scheduled to work.

- Checkouts were fully manned even though the store wasn't busy. A closer look revealed that many of the bored looking employees were from other departments.

- All managers from the other departments were on the shop floor stacking shelves etc. instead of managing their departments. This should only happen in emergencies.

- The store atmosphere was despondent and lacked vitality.

- Customers were needing assistance but couldn't find anyone on the shop floor to help.

Robert returned to his office and looked closely at the employees' working schedules, agreed overtime figures (e.g. cost and department) and store profitability.

He noticed that whilst Harry's budget was significantly underspent (namely payroll costs) it was at a cost to the Store's overall profitability. Harry was drawing employees from all over the store – thus saving payroll costs for himself and significantly increasing overtime costs for the other department heads. The Store also had empty shelves reducing the ability of shoppers to find and buy what they needed.

The Store had increased absence levels (employees were unhappy and taking time off by calling in sick, and those that had to work longer hours to cover their absence, were genuinely becoming ill and therefore taking time off work).

When Robert initially approached the Store Manager to advise that Harry was pulling staff from around the store and Robert was going to put a stop to it; the Store Manager chastised him. The Store Manager admired Harry's ingenuity in being efficient, at the expense of others. The Store Manager felt that the other Department Heads were weak as they allowed it to happen. 'Just leave it Robert', he advised.

When Robert detailed the impact to the Store profitability by quoting the actual cost in lost sales, increased overtime, and absence levels; the Store Manager was furious with Harry.

In this example, Robert the maverick, solved a problem that the Store Manager either didn't think existed or didn't care to see it resolved. He did this even though Harry was a friend of his and that the Store Manager wanted to maintain the status quo. Robert wanted to ensure that the supermarket's stated goal, to increase its market share and profitability was not compromised.

Mavericks believe in the brutal truth, whatever the cost

To the maverick's surprise and confusion, it is rare for their efforts to tell the truth, to be fully appreciated. They cannot understand why it is assumed that they are just being mean to others, when they are only trying to improve the situation, by highlighting some home truths.

'If only the Conformists took on board these truths, then there would be improvement', thinks the maverick. The Conformist's reactions confuse the maverick; surely the conformist would want to improve; they know they would if the situation was reversed.

Mavericks, being more concerned with the truth, aren't interested with other's opinions of them (unless it starts to affect what they want to do, in which case they will take steps to remedy the situation).

For mavericks, other people's opinions are just data. The maverick will not act on the opinions of others until they have processed the validity of the comments. The opinions of others, do not sway them, one way or another until the Conformist's opinions, have gone through the maverick's analytical process. The only exceptions to this, are when the maverick has received opinions from a credible and accepted source (to the maverick).

Mavericks' feelings are not hurt when they are on the receiving end of unfair or difficult criticism. In so much as, those comments will not affect the maverick's self-esteem or confidence. After all, the maverick sees this information as just data to be processed.

The maverick will analyse what they have been told and then they will decide whether they will accept some or all of what has been said. (It is to be noted that Socialised Mavericks will look at this data from all angles, to test its validity. Extreme Mavericks tend to stop this assessment if they quickly decide the other person is wrong, tending to want to rapidly remove, any cognitive dissonance they may be experiencing).

If the maverick does not accept what has been said, or presented to them, they will dismiss some or all the comments and will not be psychologically harmed or distressed too much. (If they are upset about the comments the Socialised Maverick will try and hide this distress, an Extreme Maverick is likely to explode or plot revenge). It is important to reiterate that unlike many Conformists if the maverick is upset about the other's comments; it does not affect self-esteem and might only knock their self-confidence slightly. Mavericks are always described as having a thick skin. This isn't necessarily true, as they prefer to hide vulnerability behind a stoic façade and do not let their emotions affect their ability to analyse the data presented to them.

Therefore, mavericks would prefer if people just gave them feedback and didn't pussy foot around tempering their comments with concerns that they might hurt their feelings. To the maverick this can feel like the Conformist is being disingenuous as they are not saying what they mean.

Mavericks tend to treat others how they like to be treated. Therefore, they have a propensity to give others the unvarnished truth. Mavericks prefer to receive information this way, they do not mind hearing raw emotion. They will strip the emotion out as they analyse what has been said, and then they will analyse the emotion and how that affects the data validity and the conviction, determination, and credibility of the other person. This presentation of the data is also useful in understanding what to do with the data afterwards and how to use it to influence or manipulate (depending on the type of maverick) the other person.

The maverick is genuinely perplexed that non-mavericks do not want to receive information in a similar way. Mavericks are confused that Conformists are more attached to *how* the information is delivered rather than the information *itself*. It is hard for mavericks to understand that the information will be dismissed if the packaging is not acceptable.

This miscommunication by both groups, leads to accusations that mavericks are offensive, thick skinned bullies that just like to hurt people. Constantly pointing out people's failings and vulnerabilities for sport. Whilst this can, sometimes, be true of Extreme Mavericks, very few people can be bothered to check whether this assessment of a maverick's character is in fact true, or that the maverick is just a victim of a poor delivery of the message.

The individual's assessment of the maverick's character can have an extremely negative impact on the maverick's personal relationships, careers, and their ability to engage with others or the task in hand.

Indiscriminate challenge of all things

The most dominate role that a maverick will assume in a group or team is Devil's Advocate; much to the annoyance of those around them (often because mavericks delight in this role and pose observations that are too insightful for most Conformists to accept). One of the challenges that mavericks face is that they often forget to mention that whilst they are playing Devil's Advocate, they are not actually expressing their own opinions. They are in fact just testing the information for holes or flaws in the argument. They are also testing the other person's conviction and passion for the opinion or project that they are presenting.

And just sometimes, they are playing Devil's Advocate for the sheer devilment of it. This can be either an outpouring of their playfulness or a method of influence/manipulation of a weak argument to a stronger one. If you wish to understand the secret power behind maverick leaders, it is important to determine which dynamic is taking place, and at which time.

This inability to see what the role of Devil's Advocate means to the maverick, at the time that they are playing it, can lead to many frustrations and anger on both sides. The biggest criticism that mavericks pose is that the Conformist is arguing with them on an opinion that the maverick does not (yet or at all) hold. Because Conformists become very emotionally involved in arguments (in a way that mavericks don't), they do not wait for the maverick to finish processing their own beliefs.

(A lot of processing happens verbally for extraverted mavericks as they like to indulge in overt data gathering).

Mavericks, therefore, are still in the Devil Advocate phase and has not yet, formed an opinion for themselves. The Conformist is therefore arguing a position that the maverick may not hold. This angers and frustrates the maverick as it shows them that the Conformist is either telling the maverick what they think the maverick thinks (dangerous!), the Conformist has a closed mind or is unable to let the maverick outline various aspects of the argument. Worse still, by interrupting the Devil's Advocate role they are literally stopping the maverick from being able to think. This annoys the maverick as they value and consider their problem-solving ability and analytical thinking processes, as rare and prized possessions.

Being Devil's Advocate, for mavericks, is an important test of the data that they have been presented with. They are looking for the best solution to the problem and are not interested in the status quo or what has happened before (unless they have tested the current method and are satisfied that it is still fit for purpose). Mavericks are excellent problem solvers as they tend to take a forensic unemotional approach to the data (data in this context, is not restricted to written information. It includes conversations, observed behavioural phenomena and actions, as well as omissions), that they are presented with.

Mavericks also take a fresh integrated approach to a problem, choosing to work with zero assumptions whilst they build a picture of what is *actually* happening, in any given situation. They will also canvas wide and disparate opinions from many sources to get an accurate representation of the problem.

Mavericks adore challenges both physical and intellectual ones. They will, therefore, look for intellectual challenges as a method for keeping their mind alert and exercised. These intellectual challenges will be sought from a variety of sources. For example, from books that challenge their thinking or perceptions, conversations with people that are intellectually superior or unique problems arising from others behaviour or issues that they are trying to solve.

The love of challenge may make the maverick appear to be contrary or 'looking for an argument' as they will want to debate anything and everything. This is often as a response to the real fear of intellectual boredom. When a maverick is bored, he will manufacture a challenge for himself. This can often lead to a disastrous result for the organisation, the maverick's peer group or employees.

The fact that the maverick is challenging everything doesn't necessarily mean that he hates you or wants to humiliate you. You may have impressed him, so he is testing you to see how worthy you are to receive his trust. Or it could simply mean he wishes to give his mind a workout. Mavericks know that one of the essential keys to success is to ensure their own personal growth, and the ability to view things laterally and from all angles. This will not happen with an obsessive narrow approach or a deep narrow knowledge of a subject. A deep knowledge of something can ensure expert knowledge (most mavericks become experts in their chosen field). To be able to apply that knowledge usefully you need to know enough about the touch points. Touch points are the things/subject areas that touch on your base knowledge.

For example, a good HR Manager will know the following:

- Base knowledge
- Core knowledge
- Applied knowledge

Base knowledge is all the functions and key things needed to run a HR department, (e.g. administration and core activities like Employee Relations). For example, you would expect a competent HR Manager to be able to reduce excessive absence, have a good grasp of Employment Law so that they can write policies and advise managers well. They would be able to avoid Employment Tribunals because the management team would be trained and motivated to do a good job. With base knowledge, you would expect the HR Manager to run an average department and be competent at their job. They would be the same as anyone else doing this role.

Having core knowledge would mean that this type of HR Manager would be more effective than the first. They already understand how to make a HR department run well (base knowledge). For example, having core knowledge would enable them to coach others and understand leadership theories. They understand people and their motivations and are therefore better placed to navigate the politics of the organisation for the greater good of the people and itself. The HR Manager can turn the HR department from competent to effective.

With applied knowledge (e.g. understanding how the HR department fits with the rest of the organisation and how HR can benefit it), the HR professional can take a truly integrated approach to what the company and its people want and need to succeed. Many professionals stick too closely to their very narrow expertise and as such may be a very good technical expert but is unable to give the company want it fully needs.

Of course, none of the above knowledge bases, speaks to character, which is equally, if not more so, important to technical skills. A HR Manager/Director etc. is only truly effective if they have all types of the above knowledge and a good character to match.

It cannot be ignored that mavericks value intellectual flexibility and ability; which is why they are highly dismissive when faced with someone who refuses to examine an argument, or point of view properly. Rigid, dogmatic thinking is annoying as mavericks believe that it demonstrates a lack of education (not necessarily intelligence) and willingness to be open to different viewpoints.

Mavericks are dismissive of ignorant people who refuse to be open in thought and mind. This is different from saying mavericks are dismissive of stupid people, they are not.

All types of maverick get very distressed if they are faced with lots of routine and little challenge. Socialised Mavericks will eventually choose to leave the situation that they find themselves in, (especially if they must expend more energy to change things than they think the situation warrants). Extreme Mavericks will eventually choose to get their kicks by disrupting the enforced routine and finding ways to manipulate the situation they are in to bring more challenge to it.

Either way, everyone loses.

A test of credibility and integrity

Mavericks challenge as an excellent way of testing someone's credibility and integrity. Whilst mavericks rely heavily on a 'gut feeling' they have a need to be sure of a person before they throw their loyalty at them. A maverick's loyalty is a precious thing and not given lightly. A maverick who *really* likes someone will test that person the hardest, which may seem counter intuitive. The other person can often feel like the maverick doesn't like them as they are constantly asking deep challenging questions and often appear to be quite contrary. The maverick will seek to know the character of the person well enough to be able to predict how they will behave in any given situation. They do not like to be surprised with something they hadn't previously considered.

For a maverick to 'get behind' someone or their ideas they need to know whether they (the individual) can be trusted. For a Socialised Maverick both aspects of trust need to be in play. They need to be able to be sure of the individual's integrity (this is an assessment of character and trust) and their expertise. For Extreme Mavericks, only the respect for the individual's expertise is necessary. They are less concerned about the moral dimension of the individual, this type of maverick can follow a dubious character if the following produces the results that they are after. Extreme Mavericks find it easier to withhold their essence when following others compared to Socialised Mavericks. Perhaps because it's important to withhold your essence when manipulating someone (so you don't get drawn into the other's perception and beliefs). If you are trying to influence for someone else (e.g. a manager) then you are more likely to closely align yourself with the cause (or person) as you are linking your reputation to the other person.

It is important to all mavericks that the other person is credible, especially if that person has a position of authority over them. New or inexperienced leaders, may initially find the maverick challenging. This is because the maverick's perspective dictates that if anyone is to have authority over them then they need to be worthy of them. If someone has little credibility and acts like they have, they are likely to be 'taken down' by the maverick.

Dependent on the type of maverick, this 'take down' can be quite mild. For example, subtly contradicting what the manager (or other) has said or proposed, by pointing out the flaws in a way that allows the manager to maintain their respect. Alternatively, it can be less mild, the maverick could humiliate them by highlighting their (perceived) stupidity.

All mavericks make an assessment on an individual's level of integrity before they decide whether it is in their best interests to align or work closely with them. By challenging the individual, whether this challenge is overt or covert, enables the maverick to better understand whether the individual can be trusted or is indeed trustworthy.

Once the maverick has formed an opinion on someone's integrity based on all the data available to them, including their sharp perception/gut feeling, it is hard for someone else to persuade them they are wrong. Whilst the maverick often makes swift first impressions, they will test their hypothesis for a while before determining that they were correct or not.

This hypothesis testing phase can take some time, and the individual that the maverick is assessing will be on the receiving end of a lukewarm response until the maverick has made up their mind. The maverick knows that they are influential people and therefore do not want to mislead others by forming a rash decision about a person (e.g. that a person is trustworthy) that others would follow.

The maverick is not only interested in testing the individual, they are also testing for flaws in an argument/discussion or idea/process. Mavericks never assume that something is fit for purpose nor that the correct process is already installed. This is not due to their own arrogance rather than their understanding that you need to go back to first principles before attempting to change anything. When presented with something they will ask several questions. They always look for what's happening in an argument before they become intellectually invested in it. (For example, why is someone following this line of argument, honest belief? Distraction? Arrogance/ignorance? Trying to upset the maverick or manipulate them?)

Mavericks are excellent problem solvers and often see problems as broken processes requiring a solution. When problem solving, mavericks ask for data in sequential order, challenging and testing every link in the process. By doing this they often see things that others overlooked or become aware of where the solution can be sought.

This is one of the reasons why their intentions are often misunderstood. Mavericks ask more detailed, searching questions that challenge everything that currently happens or tests the assumptions already made. The maverick's questions come thick and fast and are often uncomfortable especially as the maverick has entered analytical mode and has already separated their emotions from the problem. Therefore, it requires effort on the maverick's part to remember to check the other person's emotions, whilst they are asking them questions. Sometimes they will interrupt long explanations because they have already uncovered what they need; or the individual is on the wrong track and they want to put them on the right track to address the issue. Mavericks are dimly aware that people find this abrupt interruption or dismissal annoying but they feel that this is less important than solving the problem, especially if time is of the essence. Their questioning process is also much longer than Conformists because they test every assumption ever made.

Conformists can find this process annoying or challenging, especially if they do not trust the maverick. The maverick will always spend a significant amount of time understanding the problem before attempting to solve it. This is because the solution is often easy to find once the problem is properly uncovered.

It is an essential aspect of the maverick mindset; believe nothing, test everything.

Part 2

The competencies of successful leaders

3. Maverick (KEY) Capabilities

"We are all capable of achieving success, but the fear of failure has driven many into the habit of only wishing for it"

– Edmond Mbiaka

People seem genuinely perplexed as to why mavericks seem to be so successful and confident in what they are doing, even if the task is something they haven't done before. Mavericks are rarely (and only under extreme conditions) riddled with self-doubt. They do not understand why others would indulge in something so disadvantageous to the psyche. If mavericks are approached by people who have extreme self-doubt, they find it disconcerting. They reason that if *you* don't believe that you can do a thing, why should you expect others to believe that you can?

Mavericks do not find individuals that have extreme self-doubt as credible individuals. This is especially true if they hold a position of authority and the self-doubt relates to an essential facet of that authority. Without credibility and respect from the maverick, the leader will find it difficult to persuade the maverick to do anything that he has no initial interest in doing.

One of the reasons that the Socialised Maverick can maintain his self-belief system is his grasp of the Maverick KEYSTONE Capabilities™ [3]. These crucial 8 capabilities (Knowledge, Emotional awareness, Your vision, Self-efficacy, Trust, Objectivity, Networkability, and Engagement) are essential for

---

[3] © Maverick KEYSTONE Capabilities – Judith Germain 2013

good, effective leadership, (including self-leadership). Another important difference between mavericks and other people, is that mavericks understand that if they wish to be an influential catalyst for change then they need to nurture and develop their own leadership abilities. Mavericks do not wait for formal recognition of leadership status nor any external references to what they can do in any given environment or situation.

All good leaders have the above Maverick KEYSTONE Capabilities™ in balance. This is the reason why Socialised Mavericks are very effective leaders. Extreme Mavericks struggle with the emotional awareness and objectivity components of the Maverick KEYSTONE Capabilities™. This alone can make them dangerous to be around. It means the Extreme Maverick can persuade and manipulate without objectivity underpinning the acquisition of their goal and the willingness to care about how this acquisition affects others. The Extreme Maverick's very nature is selfish.

For Extreme Mavericks if their goal has been achieved, little else matters.

The Maverick KEYSTONE Capabilities™ are key components of success, and how the capabilities are balanced and demonstrated will determine where an individual is on the Maverick Continuum™.

I've noticed when beginning work with leadership teams or individuals who aspire to be leaders, that the biggest struggle they have, is not the leadership techniques (these are, or should be, easily learned and applied); it's knowing how to *be* a leader. It doesn't help that there are few good leadership role models to emulate.

These aspiring leaders are unsure whether they have the right internal resources and if so, how to apply them. They also struggle with knowing which leadership techniques to apply and when. Leadership should not be all about techniques, who you are as an individual and what value you bring to your followers, is highly important as well.

My belief is that all good leaders, at the very least, are Maverick Behaviourists; properly attuned and flexibly applied to the situation at hand.

Richard: *(Walks up to two of his employees who are talking around the coffee machine)* Remember our meeting at 2 o'clock? We must put together the company's vision statement. So, we will need plenty of blue-sky thinking and mind storming! I know you guys can help, you are my best problem solving employees!

(Richard leaves them and goes back into his office and shuts the door. He sighs, sits down, and swings his chair around pondering. 'Well, that was some pretty good encouraging I did there!' He thinks. 'Now they think I value their opinion and they are now ready and motivated for our 2 o'clock meeting. The meeting is really important, it's such a shame that I do most of the thinking in the department. That Peter is my most intelligent employee when I can get him to be motivated. He always thinks of innovative solutions that really make a

difference. Problem is, he spends most of the time fighting with me and not doing what I ask. I'm not sure what to do with him'. Richard sighs again, wakes up his computer and looks at his screen).

Toby: *(Toby watches Richard enter his office, closes the door, and exclaims)* Here we go again!

Peter: I know, he sounds like a complete idiot!

Toby: Every time he goes away on a training course he comes back with a lot of management mumbo jumbo and then changes everything. Two weeks later he is back to normal, changes everything back and is even worse than before!

Peter: Hmm, he couldn't lead a piss up in a brewery!

Peter returned to his cubicle thinking about the past few days in the office. When Richard had gone away for his course; everyone, not just Peter, sighed with relief. Those few days of the company running like clockwork were absolute bliss. They really didn't need much leadership as a team, just a few helpful pointers in the right direction, from time to time. Richard had a very directive style of management rather than a collaborative one.

> *But then Monday had arrived with the return of Richard, had the week away changed him for the better? Er no, he was just the same as ever. Peter sighed and woke up his computer.*

Most employees who have worked in an office will know the 'leadership training course' phenomenon. This is where an average or poor performing manager attends a leadership training course they return to the office, and for the next two weeks, spout a lot of 'management talk'. They are full of enthusiasm and attack their department like a man possessed. Then slowly, after the two weeks have lapsed, they return to their previous poor performance. Sometimes they perform even worse than before. Leadership training never 'sticks' for them, because they essentially haven't changed themselves.

This is a common occurrence on most leadership courses, as they tend to teach techniques without trying to change the behaviour (or heart) of the manager. I believe in changing behaviour and therefore design and deliver leadership courses that radically change the behaviour and effectiveness of mavericks. If you can change the maverick's mode of operation, then the same course would be a radical lasting behavioural change for Conformists also! This avoids 'the leadership training course' phenomenon.

The impact on the organisation, due to these changes would be immense.

For sustainable leadership change to work, you often need to shift the individual's leadership paradigm. It is important to start with the internal shift of the individual before you move to their external expression of that shift.

Therefore, the first place to start is by improving the individual's own capabilities.

The Maverick KEYSTONE Capabilities™ are listed below:

- **K**nowledge
- **E**motional awareness
- **Y**our vision
- **S**elf-efficacy
- **T**rust
- **O**bjectivity
- **N**etworkability
- **E**ngagement

These core capabilities are essential for maverick leadership. Maverick leadership is not just for those with formal leadership authority. It is also for those that aspire to lead in all aspects of their life.

Mavericks see leadership as a way of life, not a title

Mavericks like to follow their own path and maintain control over their environment. They like to be influential in any given situation, recognising that influence does not need the mantel of formal leadership structures. They understand that at times you can be more influential in the number two position rather than the pole position. Mavericks, especially Socialised ones are happy to occupy the number two position, if it means they are a more effective influencer in this role and they get what they want. This may mean that they show a preference for being king maker rather than king. (This has the advantage of making the Socialised Maverick less of a target).

All mavericks understand instinctively, that to be influential then you must nurture your own development. Mavericks recognise that to be successful in life they need to become leaders. They need to have a firm grasp of the principles of self-leadership before they move on to expressing their leadership capabilities to others.

Whenever a decision needs to be made, people will look for the natural leaders. If the formal leader is ineffective this can become problematic for the company. This is because your employees may look towards the maverick or Maverick Behaviourist for a solution, rather than the formal leader. Dependent on which type of maverick they turn to, it can either be detrimental or beneficial to the manager, to have them on the team.

Maverick KEYSTONE Capabilities™ works on two levels:

- Aspiring managers can nurture their Maverick KEYSTONE Capabilities™ within their organisation to develop their leadership capability. Companies can use them to vastly improve their leadership cadre

- Individuals outside of a corporate framework, can develop their Maverick KEYSTONE Capabilities™ to improve their own lives, or chances of becoming a leader/manager within an organisation of their choosing

The advantage of Maverick KEYSTONE Capabilities™ is that an individual can develop these capabilities outside of organisational frameworks if they want.

Becoming a maverick leader is about leading without formal authority. Wielding your Maverick KEYSTONE Capabilities™ is an essential life skill.

Why are Maverick KEYSTONE Capabilities™ important?

Competencies (measured by HR departments) are usually considered by companies to be specific qualities; abilities or attributes that an organisation has decided its employees must have to be able to execute their job properly.

Whenever an organisation talks about competencies they are only referring to what they have deemed to be useful to them. (Ironically when organisations go through significant change, they rarely update the competencies that they assess their employees with. This means that over time the organisation will gradually be staffed by employees who are being assessed against criteria that is no longer useful to the company. This can only hinder the company's success).

Sometimes, companies only use competencies to recruit new employees. This means that there has been no attempt to embed a Competency Framework within the organisation. This makes a nonsense of company claims that certain competences are important to the company.

In any event, competencies and their frameworks are usually company structures that aren't seen as useful to an individual outside of their working life (or even within it at times). Imagine an employee whose performance review is based on their ability to demonstrate the company competencies. The individual is aware that no matter how well he performs within the Competency Framework it will not translate into a pay rise that is equitable to his actual work performance. How likely do you suppose that the employee will value the Competency Framework and seek to improve his ability within it, as his years within the company increases? (This is an example of a poor tie up of competencies and work performance).

Therefore, company competencies do not hold much, if any, intrinsic value to the employee. This is where Maverick KEYSTONE Capabilities™ differ from company competencies. They are an effective life skill useful to the employee on a personal level. The benefit to the company is that the Maverick KEYSTONE Capabilities™ are exactly what companies need from their employees to be more successful in their marketplace. It is a win/win scenario.

The Maverick KEYSTONE Capabilities™, a key to future success.

The Maverick KEYSTONE Capabilities™ are a foundational step to becoming a maverick leader. If the workforce masters these capabilities it will bring success to the organisation too. If the organisation's leaders are brave enough to accept the challenge, a win/win situation can occur.

Maverick KEYSTONE Capabilities™ are not hierarchical in nature which means that they do not need to be developed in any specific order. It is beneficial to realise that you are instead developing multiple capabilities simultaneously. This is a journey of Maverick KEYSTONE Capabilities™ mastery and as such it is impossible to announce that you are now completely proficient in all the Maverick KEYSTONE Capabilities™. The journey of mastery is never completed, because self-knowledge and the ability to translate that self-knowledge into effective action never ends.

Mavericks rarely look towards others to define who they are or what they can do. Mavericks make and trust their own assessment of their abilities. They will only seek confirmation of their own opinion from people that they trust. This is typically other mavericks or trusted sources of expertise.

Socialised Mavericks tend to score highly in self-awareness (which is a component of the knowledge capability) and are therefore able to reliably trust their own assessment. Unfortunately, Extreme Mavericks do not score highly on self-awareness due to their lack of objectivity and situational narcissism. The key to changing their behaviour is to be either a Socialised Maverick yourself or become a trusted source of expertise that the Extreme Maverick can rely on.

All mavericks, however, are internally driven and motivated, never needing an external source to validate who they are. This ability to internally motivate and drive oneself, is essential for the maverick leader especially as numerous studies show that internally motivated people are more successful than externally motivated ones.

Unless they are designed very carefully corporate reward schemes are ultimately unsuccessful. These schemes tend to skew behaviour and rewards to financial outcomes, leading to detrimental results or unethical behaviour. The numerous financial crises caused by rogue traders are good examples of this.

An individual aspiring towards Maverick Behaviourist or Socialised Maverick status could have a formal assessment of their Maverick KEYSTONE Capabilities™ completed. This would enable them to become better maverick leaders in the future. It is important to have well developed and balanced

Maverick KEYSTONE Capabilities™ as they provide the foundational framework to increase your ability to influence and lead others. Without Maverick Behaviourist or Socialised Maverick traits, the path to success (however you define success) will be more difficult and harder to obtain and keep. If you have an abundance of balanced maverick traits, then you will experience little self-doubt and negative thinking which impedes your desire and ability to be successful.

All mavericks want what they want, how they want it, when they want it. Internal motivation and mastery of the Maverick KEYSTONE Capabilities™ is an excellent first step on the pathway to success.

To be able to nurture and develop your Maverick KEYSTONE Capabilities™ you must at first understand its components. This is essential for an individual to travel the Maverick Continuum™ to either Maverick Behaviourist or Socialised Maverick status.

Maverick leadership is twofold:

- Leadership of self
- Leadership of others

Remember, maverick leadership does not require any formal recognition of leadership authority. In this chapter, we will look at the first 3 Maverick KEYSTONE Capabilities™ (KEY)

K is for knowledge

This capability component is surprisingly multifaceted.

It is easy to believe that the knowledge capability is just the acquisition and recall of facts. For example, if someone acquires an impressive number of facts about dinosaurs, you would say that the palaeontologist is very *knowledgeable* about dinosaurs. This does not mean that the palaeontologist has mastered the knowledge capability though. This is because it is important that the palaeontologist can *understand and interpret* what they have learnt as well as the recall of facts.

Real knowledge only comes from experience or modelling of someone else's experience. For example, a consultant could have a meeting with the current manager of a failing department. The manager could describe the department in enough detail for the consultant to understand how it works, the employees' capabilities and to theorise what might be going wrong and how to fix it. Whilst the consultant doesn't have the manager's experience in running the department, he now has enough theoretical experience to act as if he was the manager.

Having a lot of facts doesn't make you knowledgeable!

It is a common misconception that if someone knows a lot about something or someone they are automatically assumed to be an expert in this matter. It is often presumed that the many facts that they have accumulated, translates to deep knowledge of the subject.

David watched Rebecca approaching him with dread. She was the Project Manager responsible for the project that would eventually make the company a sizeable profit. All she ever did was 'chew him out' for not meeting the deadlines that she had set and therefore 'holding up the project'. David knew that Rebecca was not well liked and other members of the project team were unable to meet the deadlines that she had set as well. Although talking to her you would assume that it's all David's fault.

As she got closer, David sighed as he surveyed his cluttered desk and bludgeoning workload. This was not going to be an easy discussion, and he had been avoiding it all week. Eventually Rebecca stood in front of David's desk hand on hip looking at her project spreadsheet.

Rebecca: Will you make your deadline of the 10th? *(She glances up from her spreadsheet to scowl at him)*

David: No, you see ...

Rebecca: No, I don't see. What's the matter, are you just lazy? No one is taking my project seriously. No one understands how important this is. I've had enough David; I'm going to the Director on this one. I'm not going to fail my objectives just because you can't be bothered to meet your deadlines. This will cost you your bonus, maybe even your job. I'm done with your delays. *(She turns on her heels and goes)*

Rebecca heads back to her desk and pulls up her entire project plan on her computer to look at the pinch points. This project equated to a significant amount of her company bonus and she was not going to lose it just because other people couldn't do their jobs properly.

She identifies that two members of her 6-man project team are significantly behind schedule. Rebecca looks at their tasks and cannot understand why that is the case. She knows how long each task takes and has scheduled those times into the plan. She considers the facts about the project that she does know to see if there are any flaws in her project plan.

Rebecca knows how long each task takes, the skills and abilities of each project member, that she has 'buy in' from every Department Head that manages one of her team members. She knows when the project needs to be delivered and the resources needed. Rebecca knows one hundred other facts that should ensure that the project can be completed on time and to budget.

Meanwhile, David watches her leave and sighs. This is not a good day. His Department Head has reiterated again that David's priority is to his department and not to Rebecca's project. His manager feels that he has spent too long on the project and due to sickness in the department, David's talents are needed elsewhere.

Another reason for David's inability to keep abreast of the project is due to another department's inefficiency. Whilst that department has met its deadline on its due date, it has meant that David could not start his part of the project on time. The two pieces of work had an inbuilt dependency, which meant that David had only 1 week to do his proportion of the work and not the month that Rebecca had allocated him. This has a significant effect on his time and resources as well as his mood and cooperation …

Whilst Rebecca knew the technical facts of the project, such as how long it would take to achieve something; she was not knowledgeable about the project. She was not aware that she did not have 'buy in' from David's manager and therefore David was unable to dedicate more of his time and resources to her project. She also did not know that some tasks on her project plan needed to take place consecutively rather than concurrently. This had a major impact on the project and its deadlines. It was a significant oversight.

Rebecca thought that she was knowledgeable because she had a lot of facts at her disposal. However, she wasn't knowledgeable because she hadn't taken the time to understand the dependencies of the project nor did she have the awareness that David was stuck in the middle of her wanting the project done and his direct line manager forbidding him from working any more hours on the project. It was not his fault that he was unable to meet her project deadlines.

If she had a higher level of knowledge capability then she might not have made such a poor error of judgement, regarding the likelihood of the project being completed on time.

E is for emotional awareness

When Daniel Goleman's book on Emotional Intelligence came out in 1995, the concept of different types of intelligence (other than IQ), became widely known. Over time, the concept of Emotional Intelligence has become to be defined (loosely) as having the ability to manage and name emotions (yours and others).

Since 1995, there has been several opposing ideas on whether Emotional Intelligence is an ability or a trait. Despite this uncertainty, many people have tried to define, measure and improve their Emotional Intelligence hoping to improve their leadership ability.

One of the proponents of Emotional Intelligence, Dr Travis Bradberry, believes that this intelligence is made up of four core skills, that are considered under two primary competencies: personal and social competence. Personal competence is your ability to manage your emotions and behaviour and encompasses your self-awareness and self-management. Social competence is your ability to understand other people so that you can respond effectively. It encompasses social awareness and relationship management.

Similarly, to Emotional Intelligence, the concept of Social Intelligence (SI) has been available for some time. Karl Albrecht has defined SI as the ability to get along well with others, and to get them to cooperate with you. Included in this definition is the ability to understand social dynamics and how to interact with them for the best results.

You could briefly summarise the two as:

- **Emotional Intelligence:** understanding and managing your emotions; understanding the emotions of others and the impact that has on the resulting relationship.

- **Social Intelligence:** being aware of the human dynamics around you and how you (and others) have an individual impact on the human environment.

SI and Emotional Intelligence are different but complimentary to each other, as deficits in one can have a devastating knock on effect on the other. We need both models to understand ourselves and how we interact with other people. All mavericks score highly in understanding both Emotional and Social Intelligence, although Extreme Mavericks aren't as competent in utilising this knowledge as Socialised Mavericks are. This is because Extreme Mavericks are less objective and are more ruled by their emotions. Therefore, they can lack empathy when they believe they have been wronged or betrayed and will focus more on exacting revenge rather than seeking to find the cause of any misunderstanding. Once the Extreme Maverick's emotions are brought into play, mere logical argument is often not enough to pull them back from the brink of destruction (theirs or others).

This lack of control and bias in their objective thought processes, once their emotions come into play, seriously hinder their ability to utilise their cognitive understanding of Emotional Intelligence.

My belief is that there is a third dimension to understanding and deploying the emotional awareness capability. It is important to be able to take a 'temperature check' of a current situation, and then extrapolate this information along with the Emotional and Social Intelligence data that you have managed to gather. To be competent in the emotional awareness capability is to be able to do this accurately in mere seconds or minutes.

Those that have high aptitude in this capability can predict how someone will behave in the future or the likely outcome of a situation.

Why a temperature check is better than a first impression

It is oft quoted that it only takes a few seconds to make a first impression, and once that impression is made it is notoriously difficult to change it. First impressions are usually applied to people and 'temperature checks' are usually applied to the environment, the situation, or the interactions of others. First impressions can suffer from the 'halo and horns' effect and be open to unintentional bias, thus increasing their limitations. The 'halo and horns' effect is when an individual allows a good trait (halo) or bad trait (horns) to overshadow the other traits that are being demonstrated. For example, a persistent example of the 'halo and horns' effect is the adage 'all attractive people are good'.

Here are some examples of when a temperature check can be used:

- the mood of the department/company/people (e.g. are people happy, sad etc.)

- whether they (department/people) are busy or not
- whether there are any issues, hostilities, or inefficiencies in the department.

Someone who is skilled in the knowledge capability can take a temperature check quickly and unobtrusively. For example, a temperature check can be taken by slowly walking through an open plan office. Another way is to sit at a desk in an open plan office for a period of time and observe what takes place (during this time the person would be working, not just sitting there doing nothing). Finally, a more formal assessment can be made.

With practice the temperature check will be highly accurate enabling the maverick leader to home into any issues that needs addressing.

To some people this assertion sounds preposterous as it appears to rely a lot on gut feeling or instinct. It is important to remember however, that it is possible to do quick temperature checks, if the aspiring leader takes the time to build up their situational awareness and perceptions of human behaviour and motivation.

> Sean has been working at his new company, as Finance Manager, for a few days and was really settling in. He was excited at the opportunity to turn things around and

help the company grow. He had a free reign to do whatever he felt was necessary to make a difference.

Sean worked in the open plan office and sat amongst his team. Whilst he worked at his desk he took a temperature check of his department. He observed several things and was keen to test his assumptions, as the days and weeks continued.

One of the things that Sean concluded was that the Finance team was not very efficient in their dealings with people and tasks. They had a constant stream of employees who came into their workspace to ask questions and seek solutions. This 'walk by trade' bypassed their managers by going to Finance (for example asking how many days' holiday they had left from their holiday allocation. Not only was this knowledge held by their managers but the employee and the Finance professional often conducted long discussions on holiday destinations during this time). This was the first-time Sean had worked for a company that did not have a HR department. He was surprised at just how many typical HR tasks came under his remit.

The Finance team had many phone calls with managers seeking advice. At the end of the call, it was common for the Finance professional to speak to another member of the Finance department about the call. In most of these cases the Finance team member would spend time 'bad mouthing' the manager. Several members of the team would 'down tools' to partake in the conversation. This was not only inefficient but contributed to the bad atmosphere between the department and the rest of the company.

The management team often stopped by the Finance department to argue with the Finance team. Finance morale was low and it was clear that the team was not respected or liked by the rest of the company.

Judging by the questions the members of the team asked Sean, it was also clear that the level of competency within the department was quite low.
Sean knew he had his work cut out for him. On entering the department, 'first impressions' implied that the team was busy and overworked. By allowing himself to take the time to do a temperature check he could understand where the potential issues were and what he had to address. Sean had a better idea of potential priorities and where to focus as an initial starting point.

During my career, as a Senior Manager and consultant, companies often asked me to 'turnaround' specific departments or entire organisations. Unlike most senior people, I favoured having a desk in an open plan office, rather than in an office isolated from the team and the coming and goings of the department.

This desk arrangement allowed me to observe through the normal day what was happening around me. For example, I could tell:

- How busy the department was (via phone calls, made and received; chatter amongst colleagues, walk by trade).

- How efficient the department was (how many interruptions, how many employees seemed to be working or making time).

- The ability of the department (types of questions asked and answered by department colleagues, or other employees).

- How the department was viewed by others (chatter about others within the departments, calls/emails received by others).

- The mood of the department (was they happy, exasperated, frustrated etc.).

One of the reasons that 'managing by walking about' is a very effective management tool is because the manager can become accessible to others and are therefore able to offer advice and support on issues as they emerge (rather than when they have been festering for some time). It can also mean that because the manager is doing 'frequent temperature checks', he can become aware of any changes in morale or other factors (such as efficiency) on the thermometer, as and when they happen. This makes him more able to provide a timely solution.

After awhile of actively trying to improve your ability to administer temperature checks, your Social Intelligence will increase as your awareness of social interaction increases. Eventually you should be able to walk into any new situation and 'sense' the 'lay of the land' with increasing accuracy. Emotional awareness is an essential survival tool enabling you to be more aware of your surroundings and current situation. Having high emotional awareness is often called instinct.

Why emotional awareness matters to mavericks

Mavericks are bemused by individuals that have a hard time saying 'no' (something that Extreme Mavericks use to their advantage on a regular basis), because they cannot imagine saying 'yes' to something that they did not want to do. Mavericks believe that they alone control what they do; which is why mavericks tend to have a heightened response whenever they perceive someone is trying to wrestle control from them.

Mavericks have a serious aversion to cognitive dissonance, so they avoid anything that may cause them to experience it. They understand that doing something that they do not want to, will cause them unnecessary internal emotional upset. Socialised Mavericks realise that if they do something that they feel coerced into doing (this includes emotional blackmail), they will feel resentful which is likely to have uncomfortable unforeseen consequences for others.

Mavericks will not voluntarily associate themselves with negative or whiny people. The reason for this is because mavericks build rapport quickly and have enough emotional awareness to be able to sense bad feelings, even if the other person feels that they are hiding their emotions well. Therefore, surrounding themselves with negativity can overwhelm the maverick emotionally, making them less effective in the present and perhaps the future. Another important reason for avoiding negative people is because of the impact that associating with them have on the people that are observing the maverick.

Chronically negative people can make the maverick look less 'attractive' and can seriously affect their referent power. This may or may not be a problem dependent on the maverick's objectives; it would be foolish to assume that this isn't something that they would have considered.

Socialised Mavericks can detach their emotions so that they think clearly and analyse data correctly. They then use their emotional awareness to consider the emotions of the those involved and the social dynamics of the situation. Only then, will there be able to make a reasoned argument or assess accurately what the next step should be. Extreme Mavericks find it hard to keep an emotional distance from a problem if they have a personal stake in it and their sense of justice and fair play has been activated.

It is easy to assume that the emotional awareness capability has entirely positive applications. However, I believe that it has a certain neutrality when considering its ability to be utilised towards others. Humans are highly emotional animals who often allow their emotions to cloud their judgement. This leaves them open to influence or manipulation. I believe that the ability to master this emotional awareness capability can demonstrate a moral divide between Socialised and Extreme Mavericks, and therefore means it can be used for the good or ill of others. Extreme Mavericks are less concerned by their own behaviour, which is why they may be great strategists on how to use their emotional awareness to manipulate others, although they themselves are unable to truly master this capability. Mastery comes from knowing how to predict, understand, nurture, and control the environment around them and the people within it (including themselves).

Y is for Your vision (the maverick's)

Every maverick has a vision and is adept at painting a compelling image for others to follow. It is important to remember that the vision that the maverick has everyone following is their vision, not yours. It is important for the manager to align their vision with the maverick's, if they want their leadership to be successful and not derailed by the maverick's pursuit of their own agenda.

Extreme Maverick managers have a hard time being successful managers because they prefer a management style that has more than a hint of situational narcissism, and they surround themselves with people who will offer little dissent or challenge to their authority (situational narcissism occurs following an individual's increase in status that leads them to act superior to others). The Extreme Maverick's preference for achieving their goals regardless of the effect on others often leads them to achieving their technical management objectives and failing their people objectives. This has a disrupting effect on the workforce.

Extreme Mavericks work better in positions of specialist consulting where they can capitalise on their expert knowledge and remain somewhat isolated from others. This would not however, negate the need for proper leadership of this individual.

Socialised Mavericks make better managers and leaders than most individuals because they have superior emotional awareness and is keen to work for the greater good. They begin by assessing what the company is trying to achieve and then translating that goal into an effective vision that they can influence their employees to align themselves with. They treat everyone 'as if' they were mavericks, that they are intelligent people, who can complete the task in hand if given the autonomy and trust to do so.

Mavericks are great story tellers and can illuminate a vision so that it becomes compelling enough for others to fight to achieve it. Whilst understanding how people think and the psychology of behaviour, mavericks can transform an ineffective, disengaged workforce, to one that will fight to secure the vision for and behalf of their leader.

By getting to know their employees, their hopes, and their dreams, they can ensure that their employees are willingly aligned to the maverick's articulated vision. Eventually, with support, this strategy improves the company culture and enhances employee engagement. It also has the effect of the Socialised Maverick being blessed with the fierce loyalty of his team.

Socialised Mavericks think in revolutionary terms and then translate when needed, this revolution into evolutionary steps so that others can follow. They are aware that Conformists can find the revolutionary change that the Socialised Maverick is thinking of, as too far out of their comfort zone. Socialised Mavericks are good at 'pacing' other people so that these individuals are not surprised about what is coming next and can prepare themselves for the evolutionary leaps that they need to take. Often at the end of the journey, when the Conformist looks back in hindsight, he is surprised at how revolutionary the maverick's suggestions were and how eagerly he was to take the journey.

Unfortunately, Extreme Mavericks often get swept up with the excitement of a revolutionary change and do not provide clear steps on how to achieve this change. This makes it extremely hard for others to follow them, and risks the individual being belittled by the maverick for 'not being able to make the cut'. It can lead to the blind acceptance of the proposed change, which is dangerous as it purports that the flawed maverick, has a perfect solution.

Mavericks do not follow others blindly and have little respect for others that do. When a maverick is trying to establish their vision for others to follow, they will try to change an individual's thought processes, expectations, and aspirations, to align them as closely as possible to the maverick. The maverick considers this a natural evolution from a process that wasn't working properly to one that does. The results of this evolution can be startling to observers, especially if an individual has become aligned to an Extreme Maverick's narcissist desires and starts acting out of character.

Socialised Mavericks translate what they want (or what they see needs doing) to a recognised vision that they can align others to. Socialised Mavericks make great 'first followers' and they teach others what they need to do to follow the leader; (in this instance the 'leader' might be a person but could be the company vision, translated by the maverick). Derek Sivers popularised the idea of 'first follower' as an underestimated form of leadership. His theory is that real leadership is provided by the 'first follower' who shows others what they must do. He explains that the 'first follower' is what transforms a lone nut into a leader.

> A common problem with organisations is that they have a disengaged poor performing workforce, who do not trust the company. The usual performance management

tools do not change this status quo and the company is at a loss as to what they should do.

The organisation eventually hires a Socialised Maverick to challenge the status quo and make a difference. The first thing that the Socialised Maverick does is analyse the situation to see where the management processes are broken. This analysis will often show that the lack of trust between the workforce and the management is warranted. There is also a lack of clarity around the company vision and the measures that are needed to ensure that the company vision is achieved.

The Socialised Maverick will then translate the company vision into a vision that they can support and align themselves to. They will utilise their own leadership ability and Maverick KEYSTONE Capabilities™ to garner trust and influence with the workforce. The Socialised Maverick will lend their reputation to the company so that its vision can be implemented. They will also engender loyalty to themselves.

Over time the Socialised Maverick becomes trusted and their leadership skills begin to turn things around, to a point where morale and work performance increases. The maverick solutions that are put into place challenge the status quo across the company. It can become uncomfortable but it's a winning solution. It is at this point that the organisation usually decides that they want to rein in the Socialised Maverick. The organisation enjoys the results but does not like the change to the status quo, even though it can see that the results are good. The organisation sees the increased morale and work performance and believes that this has been caused by something that the company did. They do not acknowledge that the catalyst was the Socialised Maverick.

The organisation begins to curtail the influence that the Socialised Maverick has and start to impose unfair restrictions that have a direct negative impact on the improvements achieved. After a time, if the Socialised Maverick cannot revert things to the winning formula they will choose to leave, especially if they do not believe that the company is worth fighting for.

This departure has a devastating impact on the workforce. They realise that they were loyal to the Socialised Maverick rather than the company. They feel betrayed by the organisation and do not want to revert to how things were before the Socialised Maverick was employed. They have enjoyed increased autonomy and trust and do not want to become disengaged again. The good employees leave and the bad stay causing long term negative impact to the company.

It is important to remember that mavericks will not support a vision that they do not believe in. They are highly influential and they are effective because they engender fierce loyalty in others. This loyalty can be used or misused depending on the circumstances, environment or maverick involved.

4. Maverick (STONE) Capabilities

"If I have the belief that I can do it, I shall surely acquire the capacity to do it even if I may not have it at the beginning"

– Mahatma Gandhi

Having considered the first 3 (KEY) capabilities of the Maverick KEYSTONE Capabilities™, we will now look at the remaining 5 (STONE) capabilities.

S is for self-efficacy

Self-belief does not necessarily ensure success, but self-disbelief assuredly spawns failure (Albert Bandura). He determined that self-efficacy is the belief in one's ability to succeed in specific situations or accomplish a task. Henry Ford described it as 'whether you believe you can or you can't, you are usually right'.

All mavericks have high self-efficacy. For Conformists, this is perhaps the maverick's most admired or hated maverick capability, depending on your world view. For some, strong self-efficacy looks like arrogance, especially if the maverick is not communicating this capability in the correct way. The self-efficacy capability affords great freedom because, unhindered by doubt, the maverick can attack whatever he wishes to achieve with great gusto.

The maverick does not believe that they can do everything (although to an outsider it may look this way), the reality is that they have confidence that they can deal with any eventuality that flows from the activity that they are about to embark. This is due to them considering the possible outcomes of their endeavours, prior to starting. For them, this is an automatic analytical process whenever the maverick considers a task. It is so automatic that by the time that the maverick reaches maturity they do not even consider it a part of their thinking process. It becomes innate and they do it without consideration.

Bandura believes that individuals develop their self-efficacy capability from four main sources:

- Personal attainment
- Effective modelling of other's experiences
- Social feedback from others
- Interpretation of physiological factors

This means the self-efficacy capability can be developed relatively easily. A manager can encourage its development within the workplace; or the individual can do this independently.

The self-efficacy capability is perhaps the most important Maverick KEYSTONE Capability™ to master, as it can directly affect everything the individual hopes to achieve. It is also important for the organisation as it is a determining factor on whether the organisation will reach or exceed its goals and objectives.

Personal Attainment

This is the most powerful of the four sources because this is something that influences the individual the most. When a task is performed successfully it strengthens our sense of self-efficacy; we believe that we can achieve increasingly difficult tasks which are similar in nature.

The best way to ensure that tasks are achievable is to break the tasks into smaller steps that are relatively easy. Then concentrate on the smaller task and ignore the other tasks. A simple example is a woman giving birth. Rather than consider the entire labour process with the potential of hours of painful contractions ahead; she can break it down to the consideration of one contraction at a time. One contraction lasts a minute, so she focuses only on getting through one minute at a time. She becomes successful at managing several minutes of painful contractions and realises that she can manage the labour process. Numerous small successes increase her self-efficacy, and her self-belief that she can achieve overall success.

Mavericks tend to have high self-efficacy levels because they have had several successes in their lives, and have been nurturing for years the belief that they can do anything that they set their mind on to achieve.

This self-belief began in early childhood either by a deliberate 'positive attitude environment', set by their parents or school; or early experiences forced onto the child where there were no other options available, other than success. For example, it is not unusual for these children to be thrust into a (leadership) position of being responsible for younger siblings, whilst the parents are unavailable.

Early and sustained levels of success influence your self-efficacy beliefs. Whilst not all the children with early leadership responsibility will grow up to be mavericks; all mavericks will have had early leadership experiences.

They are usually right in their self-belief.

Individuals that fail consistently have low self-efficacy and this can have huge implications for organisations that wish to become more successful and profitable. Conformists with low self-confidence will not push boundaries and take risks; even necessary risks that would radically change the status quo to achieve better outcomes for everybody. In fact, the total opposite may take place, where the Conformist will stifle creativity and risk taking behaviour, even moderate ones.

By encouraging more Maverick Behaviourist behaviour and harnessing the power of the mavericks within the organisation, companies can make substantial change and innovation. They will also have more engaged employees working together for the greater good.

Effective modelling of other people's experiences

Self-efficacy can be increased by observing others performing a task successfully, especially if the individual is deemed similar to the observer. Perhaps they are of the same age or gender for example. If during the observation, the individual has struggled to complete the task and has been ultimately successful, it helps the observer to visualise their own successful completion of the task.

There is a clear difference between Conformists, Maverick Behaviourists, and mavericks when it comes to modelling behaviour; Conformists aren't as good at it. This, unfortunately, reduces the modelling source as an effective method of increasing self-efficacy for them. Conformists tend to be more passive in their observation than the other two types of individuals, asking shallow questions which robs them of the richness of the experience.

Mavericks (including Behaviourists) due to their keen observation skills, questioning technique, and analytical mindset, can model successful behaviour or avoid unsuccessful behaviour easily.

Social feedback from others

When an individual has been encouraged by others, self-efficacy increases; and is usually reduced when they have been discouraged. The overall effect that social feedback can have on an individual will depend on their personality. Due to a maverick's wilful intention and honest belief it is unlikely that discouragement will hamper their self-confidence. It is likely to have the opposite effect, having provided them with something to fight against, it may in fact improve their performance and determination.

Interpretation of physiological factors

How an individual interprets and reacts to their body's responses will have a significant impact on someone's self-efficacy. Mavericks almost always interpret 'butterflies in their stomach' as signs of excitement rather than signs of distress. This increases their ability to perform and increases their self-efficacy. Those that interpret their body's reactions as a distress response will have lower self-confidence and poorer performance.

T is for trust

The need for trust in your leader is self-evident, although the following is worth noting:

Without trust you cannot have leadership, and all mavericks are experts at getting people to trust them; although their methods will differ depending on the type of maverick involved. One of the biggest challenges facing companies right now is a crisis of leadership; which is caused in part by the inability of individuals to lead and the lack of trust employees have in their leadership. Good leaders are role models and are strong empathic characters that demonstrate high emotional awareness. They are trusted and trustworthy (like Socialised Mavericks).

Effective leaders are trusted, but not necessarily trustworthy (like Extreme Mavericks). Trustworthiness includes traits like integrity and character. Being trusted involves an awareness that someone will deliver what they say they will and have the competence and track record to carry it out.

To help develop trust in the leader, the leader must provide the right level of autonomy to his employees. A leader that has an inappropriate command and control style of leadership demonstrates a breath-taking level of distrust in the employee's abilities. This will encourage the employees to reduce their work performance and be less likely to be loyal to the manager or their company.

Credible leaders will be an expert in what they do, demonstrating a track record of competence that enables others to have confidence in their ability.

O is for objectivity

All mavericks have the capacity to demonstrate extreme objectivity which enables them to analyse almost flawlessly and detach emotion from their decision making. However, whilst Extreme Mavericks can show this objectivity, it is only for a short period, on a narrow subject of interest. This is because their biggest flaw is their extreme emotion which gets in the way of their objectivity. Unlike Socialised Mavericks that like to keep their maverick attributes in balance, Extreme Mavericks will give more credence to the attributes that fan their sense of self-righteousness or acute sense of justice.

Extreme Mavericks are always looking for a crusade to lead and a revolution to die for.

They do not have the incisive self-awareness (Emotional and Social Intelligence) that Socialised Mavericks have, so they only have a dim awareness that their objectivity is flawed. The attributes that mean more to them than their objectivity attribute are as follows:

- Wilful intention
- Honest belief
- Execution and output driven
- Success driven

The other attributes have equal or similar credence to objectivity. Extreme Mavericks are charming, influential people that can manipulate others to get what they want or to play a game of their own choosing. This manipulation is often behind the scenes and is subtle. If you do not look for it, the manipulation can be missed. After all these mavericks are a good study of human nature and is acutely aware of what drives others. Unfortunately, they are often blind to what drives themselves or deliberately unaware as they do not want to focus on anything that will take them away from their chosen goal.

Extreme Mavericks are very loyal to their supporters. Therefore, if 'one of their own' is in trouble, then they will 'go all out' to protect them. They will put aside their objectivity and focus on attacking their friend's enemies to ensure that their friend wins. With little morality on their side they will attack an individual to either distract onlookers or destroy the individual's will; if this is the only way to ensure that their friend is 'safe'. They have no concern about what is the objective truth of the situation is, the only 'truth' that they are interested in is that their friend needs help and they can provide it. The Extreme Maverick will throw *all* their resources at their friend's problem even though they know that their friend is in the wrong. Loyalty to their friend tops all considerations.

> Suzie was in trouble and she wasn't sure what to do. Charlotte had discovered that she had made a major mistake at work and had the decency to approach her about it. Charlotte suggested that Suzie stopped doing what she was doing and make amends. Although Suzie knew Charlotte would never tell anyone, she also knew that if anyone found out about her error she would lose their trust. Suzie would also lose credibility. She liked being popular and she knew that her popularity would wane.
>
> Suzie knew that whilst Charlotte would not go out of her way to tell others, she would not allow someone else to take the blame if the error became known. Charlotte was too honest for that, and she knew that Charlotte had

asked her to do the right thing because she was loyal to her friend Suzie.

In that moment, Suzie hated the good natured, popular, and honest Charlotte. She did not want to admit to her error, and lose face. She had a short time before her error became apparent and Charlotte would be forced to confirm that Suzie was at fault. Suzie knew that her friend would wait until the very last minute before telling others of her error. Suzie would use that to her advantage.

Suzie sprang into action and tracked down Brian. Brian was very popular in the organisation and was known to 'get a little crazy', when he felt threatened. He was valuable to the organisation so his position was secure. He had a large network of people and he was known to champion the underdog.

Suzie: Brian I need your help. Charlotte hates me and she is trying to pin something on me. I'm not sure what it is but I need your help.

Brian: Really? That's not like her, I thought you were friends?

Suzie: That's what I thought, but she's after me and you know how close she is to management. Can you really trust her?

Suzie spent some time convincing Brian that she was a true underdog and only he could save her. She told Brian things Charlotte was supposed to have said about him and his friends that were slanderous in nature. She explained that these lies were holding back promotions for several of his friends.

Brian wasn't sure that Suzie was telling the truth, he had known Charlotte for years and considered her a friend even though he didn't know her very well. It did not sit well with him, because the things that Charlotte was accused of was just not in her nature. He had only known Suzie for a short while, and whilst she was outgoing her true nature was unknown.

Brian knew Charlotte was friends with Bob, and he hated Bob with a passion. He knew that if he went after Charlotte, Bob would try and protect her. Brian could then legitimately go after Bob.

He pushed aside any lingering doubts that Charlotte might be innocent and started to plan Bob's downfall by attacking Charlotte.

For the next few months, the error was forgotten whilst the organisation split its loyalties between Brian and Charlotte. Unlike Brian, Charlotte refused to play dirty, even keeping Suzie's confidences that she had shared when they were friends. Charlotte watched her friendships disappear and reputation turn into tatters under the onslaught of Brian's lies and her misguided decision to take the moral high ground.

Brian's supporters believed that her decision to take the moral high ground made her look guilty. Whilst she got a lot of support from people, none of them wanted to be known publicly, fearing Brian might turn his attack onto them. She was effectively isolated and she realised that in this environment the truth didn't matter as much as the perception did. Charlotte was not prepared to stay in the company in which she felt betrayed. She was well known and had a reputation for honesty and integrity. Charlotte thought that the other employees should have given her the benefit of the doubt before they had sided with Brian, who was known to twist the truth on occasion. She felt that people should have had a stronger moral backbone. Charlotte was disgusted and decided to leave the organisation.

As she was making plans to leave, the truth about Suzie became known and it became clear that the attack on Charlotte was unfounded and unnecessary.

The damage had been done though and Charlotte learned a valuable lesson, not least that Extreme Mavericks will throw out their objectivity if they have something else that is important to them, that they wish to gain. For Extreme Mavericks, the ends always justify the means, without exception.

Troublesome Talent® in the workplace are Extreme Mavericks with often flawed objectivity, that have chosen not to continue their journey on the Maverick Continuum™. They have chosen not to become Socialised Mavericks.

N is for network

All mavericks can network well and will have a useful number of connections. Extraverted Mavericks will have a large network, having 'collected' an eclectic and diverse group of people (they love the discourse from lots of different people). Introverted Mavericks will have a small, focused number of connections pertinent to what they are currently doing. It is common for an introverted maverick to drop these connections when they move onto something different, preferring to make new connections pertinent to their current interests.

Both Socialised and Extreme Mavericks understand the need to cultivate an effective network of people that will be helpful in the future. This does not necessarily mean a network of people that the maverick can 'use' to obtain something they want, (certainly the Socialised Maverick is not as mercenary as that). This network will include people that can enhance their power bases. For example, the right people can help the maverick achieve expert power or assert more influence.

Mavericks have a great sense of timing, so they can nurture and develop networks easily, knowing when to make that call to 'touch base' or see if they can provide assistance. Mavericks are naturally charming which means that people are genuinely pleased to hear from them and trust them easily.

To most company professionals the term 'networking' is assumed to relate to the activity of external consultants who need to network to find work (or the company sales people). Networking isn't something that 'internals' think they do or indeed need to do, to survive in their organisation or improve their work performance. This is a dangerous assumption, which mavericks never make, especially in a recession where ability to perform well in your role is an underlying expectation of competency. Internal professionals need to be far more than just competent. The ability to build and nurture relationships, have advocates, build reputation, demonstrate credibility, openness, and trust, as well as having fantastic interpersonal skills, is a survival technique. This is everything that a good professional networker takes for granted.

Mavericks enhance their credibility and effectiveness by networking across the organisation as well as external to it. They are always surprised that many other people choose not to do this, but sees this reluctance as an advantage to them.

Why are non-mavericks reluctant to network?

There is a myriad of reasons why there may be a disinclination to network, especially outside their department. Sometimes it may be due to stepping outside comfort zones especially in what appear to be closed environments, where they do not have the expertise to dominate the conversation. This fear of looking stupid may dissuade them from corporate networking. Mavericks find these environments invigorating and understand that if they can master them, then their influence will increase.

Sometimes there is so much work to do that leaving the office, just to network, can be perceived as a waste of time and valuable resource. A Socialised Maverick can sense the 'temperature' of an organisation before the evidence filters through official channels. This gives him an edge and can facilitate cooperation and collaboration across departments through the maverick's ability, amongst other things, to be the conduit of information and understanding of behaviour. The Socialised Maverick's excellent interpersonal skills enable them to assist others in meeting their objectives, build a good reputation for themselves and enable the business to increase its performance. This has the added benefit in enhancing their ability to influence.

E is for engagement

The term engagement is so over used in organisations that many people switch off when they hear it. This is because when most companies talk about engagement they really mean, 'how do we get employees to do more, seem interested in their job, without significantly changing what we are currently doing?' For lots of employees, the term engagement usually means that the company is going to do something to them, rather than do something for them. Employee engagement is a workplace approach where the organisation provides the environment for people to do their best. Both the employees and the organisation need to fulfil the two conditions required for employee engagement; integrity and trust. This is where the scepticism normally creeps in, companies usually struggle to show integrity or allow employees to trust them.

This is where Maverick Behaviourists and Socialised Maverick leaders differ from other leaders. They understand that they cannot usually control how the company portray themselves or whether they have integrity or trust as one of their attributes. They, therefore, work towards enabling their employees to be engaged with them directly. This has the advantage (to the organisation) of ensuring that they get the best out of their employees. It has the disadvantage of having several employees who are loyal to a manager and not the company. If the manager leaves or becomes disillusioned, then the company risks despondent or disengaged employees that are keen to leave. Often companies fail to notice that highly engaged employees are loyal to their manager and not the company. They count on this engagement and make lofty strategic goals concerning them. Their plans are however, built on sand, collapsing if the manager leaves or becomes disillusioned. This misunderstanding of the manager's role becomes possible, because good managers praise their staff and are supportive and discusses all successes as what the 'team did' and all failures as what 'they did'. Many companies fail to see that this method of leadership works because of the manager's leadership ability. After a time, they believe that they do not need this manager as the team is doing all the work. This is an incorrect and dangerous assumption.

Maverick Behaviourists or mavericks do not need to be in a management or leadership position to understand the need to have their co-workers engaged with them. They attempt to engage with everyone. Having a network of engaged and loyal people increases the maverick's influence and effectiveness as well as enjoyment in the job.

Mavericks are natural hub and spokes people (they are the hub and the others the spokes) rather than top down people (who sit on the top and push information downwards. This 'hub and spokes' preference is a more effective model.

Mavericks study people and as such find it easy to understand what people want and what motivates them. They immediately sense others vulnerabilities and choose minute by minute whether to use this knowledge in a kind or damaging way. This is what can make mavericks awe inspiring or dangerous depending on how they use this knowledge.

Mavericks can see right into your soul and give you what you need or take it away.

Socialised Mavericks work hard to not abuse this knowledge whilst Extreme Mavericks file it away for future usefulness. All mavericks know how to engage others and how to gather loyal people around them. Extreme Mavericks do it consciously and Socialised Mavericks do it subconsciously, they engage others naturally by dint of who they are.

Mavericks get to know the people that surround them, they have a genuine interest in people and the puzzle that they represent, so they enjoy learning about the individual. They will not waste time asking you questions like 'do you have any brothers or sisters', (they assume that if it's important to you, you will tell them. They prefer to ask you questions that disclose your thinking process or things that go to the core of who you are).

If a maverick shares his mind with you, he considers it a deep level of intimacy and shows that you have reached their exclusive inner circle. This is the reason that mavericks tend to ask deeply personal questions about the people that they are keen to know. They are trying to determine if one day they will let you into their inner circle. This is also why mavericks will share the conclusion of their deliberations but not how they reached their conclusions. To understand how they think gives you an advantage over them and makes them vulnerable to you. This vulnerability is something that they only allow on a few rare occasions.

Mavericks are very motivating individuals and are happy to share their knowledge and expertise in developing others. This is endearing, and helps them to become loyal to the maverick and become an important connection to them. Socialised Mavericks like to develop others because they do not like people to be too dependent on them; as they feel this restricts their freedom and autonomy. They also believe that this dependency is damaging to the individual overall.

The ability of the maverick to make individuals feel like they are special and interesting enables them to become a hub of information and gather loyal and interested (in them) supporters (spokes). It makes their influence (or manipulation) easier and therefore naturally extends their leadership ability. Mavericks genuinely care for people, so their interest isn't faked and for those that they like and respect they will have a loyal and worthwhile ally in the maverick. It's a symbiotic relationship as the individual needs the maverick's care and attention and the maverick needs the loyalty and adulation. It is worthwhile remembering though that Extreme Mavericks will sever their ties with individuals if their utility wanes and they are no longer useful to them.

Here is a useful summary of the Maverick KEYSTONE Capabilities™:

Capability	Extreme Maverick	Socialised Maverick
Knowledge	Highly knowledgeable	Highly knowledgeable
Emotional awareness	Finds it hard to keep emotional distance. Objectivity compromised by emotions	Finds it easy to keep emotional distance. Objectivity used to make accurate analysis
Your vision (the maverick's)	Maverick's narcissist vision achieved regardless of consequence. Revolutionary change	Maverick's vision achieved by influencing others, vision is always for the greater good. Revolutionary change converted to evolutionary change for others to follow
Self-efficacy Trust	High self confidence. Requires associates to be loyal to him. Unconcerned whether associates have integrity. Is considered trusted by associates	High self confidence. Requires associates to be trustworthy. Values integrity and character. Is considered trustworthy and is trusted by associates
Objectivity	Emotion effects objectivity. Interested in (their) relative truth only	Detaches emotion to be objective. Actively seeks other views or resources to maintain objectivity
Network	Effective networks for their purposes	Effective networks for their purposes
Engagement	High ability to ensure others engage with them. Will sever ties if it's more beneficial to focus elsewhere	High ability to ensure others engage with them. Will sever ties if individual has integrity issues, otherwise they will maintain engagement even if individual's utility wanes

© **Maverick KEYSTONE Capabilities™ Chart – Judith Germain 2016**

Part 3

The use of power by successful leaders

5. Harnessing Maverick Power

"'Doublethink' means the power of holding two contradictory beliefs in one's mind simultaneously, and accepting both of them"

– George Orwell

If the definition of power is the ability to change the behaviour of others, then all mavericks exert power in their day to day dealings. Whilst leaders wield power, it is foolish to believe that leadership and power is the same thing. Leadership is about the leaders and the followers (what they need and how they work together) and power is all about the individual (their needs and how others can fulfil them).

Socialised Mavericks tend to use power carefully, being aware that having 'great power leads to great responsibility', and try hard to use their 'great power' for good. Extreme Mavericks have no such compunction. They are happy to use their ability to manipulate hand in hand, with their ability to exert power. This is one of the reasons that they can be so intimidating to others.

Whilst there are many different bases of power (legitimate and personal), we will consider French and Raven's Five Forms of Power, as they are the most well-known and recognised:

1. **Positional Power**

   This is when it is believed that a person has the right to make demands of you based on the position that they are holding (e.g. police officer, manager). It is expected that you will comply with those demands to the best of your ability.

2. Reward Power

When you have this power, you can a reward someone who complies with the demands that you place on them. It is often used to support legitimate power. Whilst the reward is often financial it does not have to be, social rewards can be compliments or flattery or even things like the best seat in the office.

3. Coercive Power

This power is about the belief that non-compliance can and will be punished. Managers often use positional, reward and coercive power together to ensure that their employees comply with their demands.

4. Referent Power

This power is all about an individual's belief that the leader has the right to your respect, or you are attracted (this includes but is not limited to physical attraction) to them. For example, this attraction can be a physical attraction or be based on how similar the other person feels to you. Referent power is also character driven (honesty and integrity can be key components) and is personal rather than legitimate power. This base is powerful because people need to identify with people of attractiveness and/or influence.

5. Expert Power

The leader's impressive knowledge and skill base generates this power. The person who has expertise power may not have high positional power but they do have expert knowledge that others need and cannot do without.

Following the formation of the 5 forms of power, Raven later added the additional power base, Informational.

6. Informational Power

This power is the most transitory in nature and originates from an individual's ability to control the information that other people need to complete their tasks. This information is general in its nature and not niched like expert power. Anyone can have this power, regardless of their formal positions. This power is as often wielded by administrators and PAs as well as mid-level managers.

Legitimate Power

Legitimate power is only powerful if other people agree that it is. Its power relies on a social structure and is probably why mavericks are so frustrating to the established power base in organisations. This means that regardless of the maverick's actual position in the company they are likely to challenge authority because they are not interested or swayed by legitimate power in others. If you wish to harness the maverick's power, then you cannot rely on legitimate power yourself. This power base does not add to your credibility or make them respect you any more than they already do.

Whilst mavericks will use legitimate power or manipulate you into believing that they have it, they rely on their personal power to achieve things. This use of personal power is attractive to others and makes them influential, especially in the long term.

Mavericks can't be managed, they must be led.

People are, usually, conditioned to comply with authority from an early age and this compliance continues into adulthood. Mavericks are aware of this bias and consider this compliance a weakness to critical thinking. This is because when told to do something or being told something, the individual's first thought is compliance. In contrast, whenever a maverick is told to do something, their very first thought is 'why?' and when they are told something, their first thought is 'really?'.

This does not mean that the maverick is distrustful or sceptical necessarily; all it reflects is the way that they think. Mavericks naturally examine all 'data' that they are exposed to as part of their analytical assessment. It is only when this assessment has been completed do mavericks move into action. If they do not have enough information so that they can act, they will continue to pepper you with more questions. These questions become more challenging until they are satisfied that they have the answers that they need to decide on how they are going to act next.

When they stop asking questions it shouldn't be assumed that they trust or believe the data that they have been given. The only conclusion that should be made is that the maverick has come to a decision, based on the data they received. In most instances, you will not be informed as to what that decision is, although it will inform their actions from that point onwards.

Mavericks are influential people for several reasons, this influence is partly based on their intuitive understanding of power bases and how they work. Mavericks understand that in a choice of legitimate power (positional, reward, coercive and informational) over personal power (referent, expert), personal power is the more powerful and their preferred choice.

With this understanding, mavericks will concentrate on developing and nurturing expert power first. This is something that the maverick can control (they can do this themselves, without the need for others' input). They are aware that expert power is the most respected power base.

As discussed previously, mavericks will not restrict themselves to becoming an expert in a narrow field. They will look to find ways to expand this expertise from the initial narrow point until they include as many touchpoints (of knowledge) that they can. This will ensure that they are recognised as an expert and they can use this expertise to influence others.

The term 'knowledge is power' refers to both the expert and informational power bases. However, the informational power base is transitory so the power in this base is illusionary.

Personal Power

Whilst working on expanding and developing their expert power base, mavericks will turn their attention to the referent power base. By understanding exactly what their target audience wants, and giving it to them; is how the referent power base is developed.

Individuals tend to be influenced by people that they can identify with; usually there is something attractive about their behaviour or personality. Those that are described as charismatic have a lot of referent power, with many people trying to imitate them and their behaviours. Human beings have a strong need to identify with others which is the true basis of referent power and makes it a strong likelihood that mavericks will knowingly or unknowingly exploit this need.

Socialised Mavericks find referent power that is based on character as the most favourable, credible, and influential. They will, therefore, credit integrity and honesty highly and dismiss attractiveness, lifestyle, and position as a good basis for referent power.

Extreme Mavericks, however, will accept and utilise referent power any which way that they can! This means that they will work on ensuring that they are as physically attractive as they possibly can (it is an accepted fact, that physically attractive people are trusted more often than those that are not), and will align themselves with a specific group, if that group enables them to influence others; even if they don't believe in the group's ideals.

Although mavericks themselves only truly respect the personal power bases they are not immune to understanding and utilising the legitimate power bases as well. Extreme Mavericks can be quite dangerous as they will use as many power bases that they can to further their own interests and will be quite blunt with their use of legitimate power. As Extreme Mavericks, they are more interested with manipulation over influence (it's quicker to implement and can achieve results quicker), so will not hold back from coercing compliance if needed. It doesn't matter if 'only their ego is offended' (they have notoriously thin skins), or if the non-compliance or offence is very minor. If it has the potential to affect their influence or how others see them, they will 'go after you', with the same vehemence as if you had physically attacked them.

> Stuart worked in the operations team and was considered by the company as the 'go to' expert. His knowledge and experience far exceeded his manager's and he had no issue letting others know how much the company valued him and how lucky they were that he worked for them.
>
> If someone else had espoused these beliefs, then they would have come across as arrogant and detestable. Stuart didn't. He always said these things with a huge smile across his face and was an attractive, charming, cheeky chappie that people were falling over to forgive.
>
> The refrain 'it's just Stuart, he doesn't mean it', was common and heartfelt. Most people who were influenced by his expert and referent power bases, didn't notice the type of person he really was.
>
> Stuart was a winner; he was a loud extrovert and knew everybody that mattered. He had connection power and was seemingly loved by everyone. You could not fault his expertise and he had a wide cluster of groupies that wanted to be just like him. They copied his brash and at other times quietly threatening behaviour to those that didn't subscribe to his world view or were influenced by him. There were always people around who were willing to act as his 'minder' and squash any sign of 'rebellion' from others. Neither Stuart or his groupies were afraid of using 'dirty tactics' to bring down those that didn't buy into his brand of the truth.

Whilst the company had not given him any formal legitimate power (for example he did not have any position of authority), he used and utilised this power base anyway. For example, he used his expert power to shore up the perception that he had legitimate power. By condemning loudly those that did not get his agreement on projects that contained some element of his expertise, he soon became the person who directed projects even those that had little impact on him or his work. From there he manoeuvred his position so that all projects went through him. He claimed legitimate power regarding projects and eventually this was accepted.

By overseeing all projects, he increased his informational power base as he alone could see the connection between projects and the potential impact on others. He was therefore able to advise better and migrate his expert power into new areas.

Stuart could use his reward and coercive power bases to good effect as well. Whilst most of the workplace only saw the charming side of Stuart, there was always an undercurrent of fear. ('Don't upset Stuart because he will come after you'), was a common and realistic refrain. However, rather than discouraging this behaviour, it was felt that 'the person must have deserved this negative attention from Stuart'. People were secretly pleased that it wasn't them that had upset him, and would not stand up to Stuart in case they were the next people to be attacked. It was easier to pretend that it wasn't happening rather than get involved). This fear related to the fact that Stuart had no compunction with punishing people that didn't agree with him (coercive power). This punishment was 'dirty' and behind the scenes. He would start unsubstantiated but persuasive rumours about someone's character or competence. He would make it harder for them to do their job by withholding information and isolating them from their supporters. He would assess where his target was getting support and then eliminate the supporter's effectiveness. This would be done by intimidating them into silence.

Stuart would also use his reward power to reward those that complied with his expressed wishes or implied behaviour. The reward, for example, could be praise, compliments, access to his network, public support, and the absence of intimidation from Stuart. This absence was prized highly.

Of course, the majority of this behaviour was under the radar of the management team (most of the time) who could only see Stuart's success and charming nature. They did not want to see a manipulating bully or one that preyed on dissenters or weaker members of the team (and subtly discouraged any mention of his bad behaviour being brought to their attention). The good team spirit that they saw was a fallacy, and a dangerous one at that.

Socialised Mavericks set out to 'get the job done' ethically and successfully. Therefore, their use of the relevant power bases can be objectively justified and they are hardly ever fairly accused of favouritism. For example, if the Socialised Maverick is using coercive power as a form of discipline, it will be fairly and objectively applied.

One of the essential differences between the type of mavericks, is that Socialised Mavericks, unlike Extreme Mavericks, can effectively separate their personal and business personas. A

Socialised Maverick may personally dislike you, but if they happen to be in a position of authority over you, they can put this dislike aside so that they can work with you in a business capacity. At times, this can cause considerable cognitive dissonance for the Socialised Maverick, especially if the disliked person is a work colleague, rather than a subordinate. This is because there is no 'positional power' at play here, compelling the Socialised Maverick to 'play nice' with the detested employee. The only reason the Socialised Maverick is working alongside the detested person, is because the maverick has a strong sense of what defines 'professional conduct'. It would take all their belief in maintaining a moral high ground, not to slip into Extreme Maverick mode and 'punish' the detested person. Even if that 'punishment' was sorely needed and just social exclusion.

For the Extreme Maverick, the term, working professionally is a misnomer. If they do not like you they will not quietly put up with this irritation, they will 'go after you', making your life extremely miserable in the process. Therefore, their favour is often sought fervently and their excesses accepted.

If you have a Socialised and Extreme Maverick in the same team, the Extreme Maverick will always try to wrestle power away from the Socialised Maverick. They will do this because they sense that it is only this type of individual that would have the power to stop them, the Extreme Maverick, from living out their excesses and negative behaviour.

In an objective and equitable environment, the Socialised Maverick will eventually win out and this would be to the success and benefit of the company and both mavericks. In a toxic environment, the Extreme Maverick will always win out, because, unless the Socialised Maverick is pushed to extreme maverickism, they will not deploy the tactics needed to turn the situation around. They will decide to leave rather than descend to strategies that they find distasteful (unless the stakes are ethically high enough). This is to the detriment of the company although the Extreme Maverick will be ecstatic that the Socialised Maverick has left.

Most people assume that all bad behaviour is in some way 'maverick'. Whilst it is understandable that people like to use stereotypical shortcuts to comprehend others, this is dangerous when considering mavericks and the correct interventions to implement. In the work environment, incorrectly diagnosing someone as a maverick can lead to the wrong business intervention being applied and therefore upsetting work colleagues and not addressing the situation effectively.

> Consider Cynthia. Cynthia worked as the secretary to the Director, and basked in reflective positional power and wielded informational power as if it was a sword. She used coercive power against those that bypassed her 'borrowed' authority and reward power for those that supported the position that she made for herself. This is how she used the power bases:

> In terms of personal power, she had little, if any. She performed at average (sometimes below average) levels. There were many people who could do the technical aspects of her job better than her, but she was extremely good at keeping the Director isolated from others in his team by denying access to his diary, and telling him small lies about his team's effectiveness. The Director liked the idea of there being hurdles to see him as he believed it enabled his team to become more autonomous, and gave him more positional power.

She had no expert or referent power. There was nothing attractive about her personality, character, or behaviour. Behind her apparently sickly sweet behaviour was a mean spirited, manipulative woman.

Cynthia assumed positional power by dint of being the Director's secretary. She often spoke on the assumed authority of the Director, when she was in fact manipulating a situation. His team was therefore, often carrying out her orders not his, often in contradiction to what the Director wanted. He never accepted that it was his PA that was manipulating behind the scenes.

This caused a lot of unrest and distrust amongst the leadership team, hampering their ability to run the company effectively.

Cynthia used reward and coercive power to reward people with increased access and favouritism and punished them with lies, misdirection and distrust amongst the team. She was poisonous with the leadership team and therefore deadly to the company. Cynthia had an impressive ability to wield informational power.

If a member of the leadership team wanted information, they had to go through her. She had fostered an environment of distrust amongst the team so they were reluctant to turn to each other. She shored up her power base in this way.

Her power as the holder of information was phenomenal, withholding information, spreading mistrust and distrust of others, and controlling access. Cynthia felt secure in her power base.

Everyone, including Cynthia, believed that she was untouchable. The focus was on cleaning up the effects of her actions, rather than stopping them in the first place.

The first thing to do, to resolve this situation, is to remove the informational power base. By enabling the leadership team to trust each other, they could work together to lessen and negate the lies and manipulations Cynthia was orchestrating. With her control over important information lessened, her power base dissipated.

Being fearful of Cynthia, and (unconsciously) assuming, that she had the ability of a maverick meant that they weren't applying the correct intervention. Cynthia needed to be subject to correct performance management techniques, to remedy her poisonous attitude. Her manager, the Director should be spoken to, to ensure that this type of behaviour did not continue again. This would send a powerful message to the workforce.

Maverick Power

Mavericks, unlike Conformists are more likely to get what they want, when they want, whenever they want. This is because maverick power is the effective utilisation of legitimate, personal, and internal power.

Socialised Mavericks are surprised if they do not get their own way and reflect on the reasons why they haven't. For them, getting resistance is a pause for thought; they will use the opportunity to reconsider their plans, examine them from all angles and decide if they still want to go ahead. If they do, then they will seek to influence others based on the new information that they have received, being cogent of the earlier dissent.

Extreme Mavericks on the other hand would be inflamed that they have not gotten their own way. Unlike Socialised Mavericks they do not pause for reflection, other than to 'double down' on pushing through their ideas. They will be outraged that someone has the audacity to go against them and will take it as a personal affront. They will seek to punish others for their dissent, unless the person happens to have more referent power to them, or authority that they respect. They will either genuinely agree with the other person or they will seek ways to avenge themselves on the other person.

Mavericks understand power, how to accumulate it, how to use it and how to recognise it in others. They understand how people react to displays of power and will seek to manipulate that reaction. Mavericks are also excellent at developing and nurturing the power bases described by French and Raven. They have a full understanding of what they are doing and the knowledge of how to utilise the power bases, until they become an innate and unconscious part of who they are. It transforms into a subconscious part of their self-efficacy.

Mavericks are most effective when they utilise their maverick attributes and Maverick KEYSTONE Capabilities™, therefore enhancing their ability to influence the actions or behaviours of others. People can sense their power and act accordingly, even at times when the Socialised Maverick, wishes to stay in the background and allow others to take responsibility. Even when the maverick has no formal authority, others will still turn to him to see whether they have his approval for a proposed action.

Internal Power

Maverick power is not just their ability to utilise their maverick attributes and capabilities; they have an additional power base which I call internal power. Mavericks draw on this to sustain the changes, or influences that they wish to make.

It is one of the things that give mavericks such a sense of presence and authority; and makes them so hard to ignore. On the flip side, it is the presence of this power that makes Conformists misread the maverick's intentions and attitudes. Therefore, Conformists often say mavericks are intimidating, even when the maverick is not actively doing anything. So, the Conformists sense this internal power and it is this that makes them feel intimidated and uncomfortable.

When necessary, or even for amusement, the maverick will 'dial up' this internal power to affect the other person on a subconscious level; therefore, making them easier to influence or manipulate when the time comes.

The internal power base has three components:

- Body Language
- Emotional Resilience
- Self-determination

Body Language

It seems that everyone considers themselves a body language expert and most people have read a book, article or watched a short video on body language. Therefore, they believe that they can read a person very easily, and can understand what they are thinking or the reasons for their behaviour.

Simple observation shows that this is not at all true, and most people cannot read beyond a few isolated body language poses (which often leads to the wrong conclusion). For example, most people would suggest that arms folded across the body, means an individual is defensive, when an observation of the body cluster (of body language poses), may indicate that the individual is just cold or disinterested! The major difference between Conformists and mavericks when it comes to observing the body language of others, is the reason why they do it.

Unless it's a survival imperative, Conformists observe others' body language in a cursory way. Mavericks will observe others' body language in the same way as a scientist observes an interesting lab animal! Mavericks are looking for insight into the individual's thinking so that they can predict how they are going to react or behave. Mavericks make a study of people so that the maverick can become better influencers as time goes by. They are also looking at inference from 'cause and effect', if I do this, they do that. 'What could this mean?', the maverick asks themselves.

It is not unusual for mavericks to replay conversations or scenes in their head, honing in on tone inflections and body language gestures/changes to assess the validity of the maverick's earlier assessment or find out what the other person really meant or thought at the time. We've already discussed how mavericks detach their emotions to analyse the data that they receive. This is another example, of how analysing the non-verbal responses they can determine the 'truth' of the matter.

Mavericks are not only good at observing body language they are very good at using their own body language to send a non-verbal message to others. Socialised Mavericks would have made a study of body language to ensure that they understand it and that they know how to use it effectively. For them it is an important power base for influence and they would take the time to understand it's nuances and would experiment with their burgeoning knowledge.

Extreme Mavericks already know the body language of intimidation and can read the subtle fear responses of others or their signs of deference and submission. In fair and objective environments, they fear Socialised Mavericks because they sense that this type of maverick understands exactly the Extreme Maverick's motivations and the interventions that they are making, to ensure that they get their own way. Socialised Mavericks will not put up with any of the Extreme Maverick's distraction techniques nor will they put up with their tactics. Because Socialised Mavericks are objective, they are more likely to out manoeuvre the Extreme Maverick. In environments like this, Socialised Mavericks are like Kryptonite to the Extreme Maverick, who will use everything in their power to discredit the Socialised Maverick, so that others will ignore or distance themselves from the Socialised Maverick. The Extreme Maverick will stop at nothing to enforce this, including defamation, dirty tricks, and manipulation.

In environments where the Extreme Maverick can be king without any obstruction, then the Socialised Maverick will struggle, unless they decide to become more extreme in their nature to best the Extreme Maverick. They will resist this, for as long as possible, (including taking the option to leave) as they do not want to 'come down to the Extreme Maverick's

level'. The Socialised Maverick will almost always opt for the moral high ground, unless they are pushed to the extreme.
Emotional Resilience

People are resilient if they can 'bounce back' quickly from setbacks. Mavericks are intrinsically motivated and as such are determined to complete the goals that they set themselves. Because they do not consider that others' thoughts or opinions are more important than their own, it is not easy to dissuade them from the path that they have set themselves. They have high self-efficacy and emotional awareness so they are not affected by the toxic thoughts of others, or their own negativity. They believe that they control the environment around them, internally and externally. If they have honest belief that they can and should do something, then it would be very hard to deter them from completion. They will not allow themselves to self-sabotage either.

'If something needs doing, something needs to be done' – a maverick mantra.

The great secret that mavericks know is that resilience can be taught, it is not something that you are born with. In fact, if you have lived a charmed life without much to test you, then you may reach adulthood without the ability to be resilient when real 'trouble' occurs. Therefore, such individuals turn to things like alcohol or drugs to medicate themselves with when life deals them a bad hand. They do not look to others for support, nor do they have internal resources to draw upon.

Mavericks, however, tend to have an engaged network of supporters around them which helps them become more emotionally resilient. They never need to face anything alone and have plenty of people around them to bounce ideas off or talk through any issues that they may have. Whilst they may not accept any advice, they will consider the solutions or points of view offered, and will feel supported by dint of the discussion that follows.

Mavericks believe *'that which does not kill us makes us stronger'* (Friedrich Nietzsche) and will look for opportunities to strengthen their adaptive skills and self-regulatory capabilities. They know that setbacks are temporary and are changeable, preferring to consider change as a learning intervention, a time to develop new skills and exploit opportunities. Individuals who are resilient tend to have strong centres of faith, hope or cultural traditions that they can utilise as supportive measures. Mavericks are no different to others in this respect.

Diane Coutu, found that there were three concepts that underpinned emotional resilience:

- Facing down reality
- Search for meaning
- Ritualised ingenuity

Mavericks could be described as optimistic pragmatists, they are optimistic about how they will respond to unexpected challenges and they believe that they have the resources to survive any hardships that the universe dares to throw at them. Mavericks believe that change is a fact of life, and that they can survive change and transform it to provide opportunities that they would want to utilise.

They put their self-efficacy capability to good effect. They are also pragmatic of the changes that they see before them. Whilst they may theorise as to why something has happened, unless it is vital to the decision-making process, they will save this type of analysis for a more opportune time. They will concentrate on what needs to happen next. They accept that change has happened and will move onto the vital next steps that need to occur.

They do this without the impediment of emotional distress at the change, proposed or otherwise. Mavericks like to be prepared so they consider what could go wrong, and how this could be remedied. This is an important part of their initial planning stage.

Mavericks never see themselves as victims because they feel in control of their world. Therefore, when something happens they do not ask 'why did this happen to me?', they ask 'why did that happen, and what should I do next?' mavericks will seek meaning for the things that happen, and if they cannot find one readily, will assign their own meaning to the event. Resilient organisations and individuals have strong values (which may be either positive or negative in their outcomes). These values enable the maverick to see the changes that occur as external to themselves, rather than because of them. For example, a redundancy would likely be perceived as an outcome of poor market conditions rather than due to the maverick's poor performance.

One of the traits that mavericks have, is their ability to make do with whatever is at hand (ritualised ingenuity). Ritualised ingenuity is having an ability to think creatively, to improvise a solution to a problem without recourse to the proper resources. Like Dory in 'Finding Dory', mavericks believe that 'there is always another way'; and will work hard to find it.

Self-determination

Mavericks understand that self-determination, like emotional resilience, can be developed. Edward Deci and Richard Ryan developed self-determination theory. They believed that people needed to feel the following to become self-determined and be intrinsically motivated:

- Competence
- Relatedness
- Autonomy

All three components need to be in place if you expect your maverick to work at peak efficiency. Mavericks will never work solely for extrinsic rewards beyond a short period of necessity. You might get their time but you will not get their hearts nor the utilisation of maverick power towards your endeavours.

Competence in this context, is the desire to control and master the environment and outcome; which is an innate need for mavericks. This is the reason some companies struggle with their mavericks, as they often refuse to let the maverick (at least in the first instance) redesign the environment to improve the likelihood of success.

Relatedness here is the need to feel that we belong. Mavericks will always have their own loyal tribe. These are individuals that respect, protect, and carry out the desires of the maverick. They care for him and he cares for them; he is their Alpha.

Autonomy relates to the need to be in control of your life, being able to act out your own values and interests. Mavericks belief that they have a free choice in what they are going to do next. No one can make them do anything, they may however allow someone to (temporarily) determine what they might do next. They always reserve the right to ignore anyone that expects them to deviate away from their principles or value system. Even if this would cost them their job. This is quite different from Conformists who are always worrying about what other people think or are keen to do whatever is expected of them.

Most managers choose to use extrinsic motivation (behaviour that is driven by external rewards, e.g. money), with their employees because it appears to be easier. For short term goals, this may work adequately, however the more that you motivate someone extrinsically the more likely that they will only work for the reward. If the reward is removed the motivation to achieve goes away as well. It is also more likely that it would be difficult to get an individual to do new or additional work without negotiating a reward.

Intrinsic motivation relates to behaviour that is driven by internal rewards. Whilst the maverick will work for extrinsic rewards he needs to be highly intrinsically motivated as well. The maverick will do something for its own sake not because there is an external need for it. For example, a maverick enjoys learning new things for the sheer love of learning and completing new challenges, not because they have an immediate need to know something.

Here's a reminder of the key components of Maverick Power:

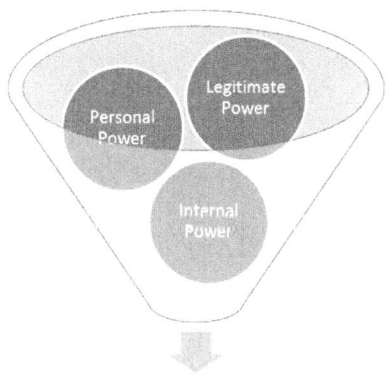

(Diagram: Personal Power, Legitimate Power, and Internal Power combining to form Maverick Power)

Maverick Power

© **Maverick Power – Judith Germain 2016**

How managers harness the maverick power of their mavericks

An overview

Mavericks are aware of the power that they wield and as such are reluctant to use this power for just anyone. Extreme Mavericks will only consider using their maverick power if they will receive sufficient personal gain (this does not necessarily mean financial, influence may be an acceptable currency). Socialised Mavericks are willing to lend their maverick power to a good manager or leader especially if they believe in and respect them.

Even if the maverick is not prepared to lend their maverick power to their manager, they will still perform well for them if treated properly. Managers are often confused or oblivious as to how they can harness maverick power. They believe that their positional, reward or coercive power will be enough to ensure that the maverick will work for them in the manner that the manager is expecting.

It's a common belief that managers need to manage everyone in the exact same way for the sake of consistency and fairness. Whilst this view is incorrect and ineffective most of the time, it is 'fatal' when applying to mavericks, especially Extreme Mavericks. If you treat mavericks in the same way as everyone else, then you are likely to manage a department that is full of disruption and resentment; usually caused by the actions of the maverick himself.

To effectively harness maverick power, from the perspective of a manager, you will need to follow the seven guiding principles below:

Lead not manage

The terms leading and managing have almost become interchangeable which has meant that many people are uncertain of what the terms mean or how they differ from each other. Worse still, the concept of managing tasks, can be lost as individuals see the term 'manage' as something that relates to a manager in an organisation. This can lead to a submissive, apathetic workforce who are always expecting 'someone else' to make the decision in their working lives.

The same can be said for the concept of the leadership team. Many organisations really mean the management team because their formal leadership team isn't, in fact, leading anyone anywhere! Small companies often suffer from the Directors managing the company rather than directing the workforce. This confusion of the roles, Director, Manager, leader can have a significant impact on the workforce and the efficiency of the organisation, regardless of its size.

Despite the terms manager and leader being used interchangeably, there is a distinct difference between the two. It is fair to say that when it comes to task management, managers will tell you what to do, and how to do it and leaders will tell you why you need to do something and leave it to you to determine what needs doing and how. You can be a leader anywhere, but you need positional power to be a manager. Since childhood, mavericks have been leaders, which is one of the reasons they remain frustrated at management. They have been leading for a long time and are more astute with the psychology of behaviour. Management can often be uninspiring and ruled by too much bureaucracy.

Mavericks do not like managing people, they would prefer to lead them. They do not want to be concerned with the minutia of their employees' day, fully expecting them to be responsible enough to get on with things or request help if they need to. This preference pervades their whole life, for example a maverick parent would lead their child, providing them with the 'why' and giving them the freedom to work out what needs to be done and how. They do this because they believe that this methodology provides excellent practice for adulthood, as well as building leadership skills. The only difference between a Socialised and Extreme Maverick in terms of them leading or managing others, is the degree of control that they will exert over the task that needs to be performed.

> Suzanne had just joined the company and had two managers reporting to her. Each manager was responsible

for distinct parts of the workload, with the most senior manager being responsible for one member of staff and the other responsible for five members of staff.

Suzanne liked all her employees to have autonomy and responsibility. She had become increasingly aware that the previous manager had a very autocratic style even resorting to 'marking' her managers' work with a red pen. This led to a disengaged team, laziness, poor self-efficacy, and low expectations from the employees.

It was also affecting the quality of work that the department was producing and Suzanne's own workload as she couldn't trust the managers to produce work that the department could be proud of.

One day, Suzanne asked one of her managers to investigate a situation that kept recurring and produce a report for discussion. When Suzanne read the report, she wanted to cry. Not only was it badly produced (e.g. spelling mistakes and formatting), there wasn't any conclusions or recommendations and the report appeared to follow an incorrect premise. This was at odds from the manager's obvious intelligence and experience. She suspected that, rather than inability causing the poor report, it was more probable that she was used to producing poor work for management review. Suzanne called Julie over to her desk.

Suzanne: Hi Julie, I just read your report. Are you happy with it?

Julie: *(Shrugs)*

Suzanne: I'm a bit surprised really.

Julie: Oh? Didn't you like it? Did you correct it yet? If so give it back to me and I'll make the corrections.

Suzanne: Well I could do that, but then I would be treating you as if you are a secretary rather than a manager and I'm not keen to do that. You see, I'm used to people giving me their very best work. Is this your best work? If so, I think we should sit down and go through it? *(raising a quizzical eyebrow)*

Julie: *(Looks at Suzanne, holds out her hand and then takes the report. She turned on her heel and walked to her desk)*

Suzanne: *(Smiles and says nothing and returns to the workload on her desk)*

Three days later, Suzanne receives an email from Julie containing the report. It is an excellent improvement and worthy of discussion on how to implement the recommendations. Neither of them discusses the first report, and word has spread. From that day on, Suzanne always received the 'best work' from her employees. This didn't mean that the work didn't need correction from time to time, but the department no longer expected Suzanne to 'mark their work' or do the thinking for them.

Morale improved immensely and so did the engagement of the employees.

Almost all employees hate to be micro-managed, however mavericks are far more sensitive to being managed than most employees. Mavericks do not relinquish control very easily (it is having control that makes them so successful), nor do they like to think that others believe that they are stupid or incapable. When they are micro-managed, the manager retains excessive control. He reduces the maverick to a mere robot who must fulfil tasks in an exact way without the freedom to think for himself or design a better solution or process. For the maverick, this is hell and soul destroying and will cause severe cognitive dissonance. This is because it is work without challenge or freedom, which is very demotivating. This is guaranteed to ensure that the maverick will fight back to reassert control of their work environment or provide interest to their role. This can have a disruptive effect on others.

When a maverick believes that others feel that he is stupid he takes it as an affront to his intellect. This will cause him significant cognitive dissonance and he will reduce it by changing the way he works, even if that means not working as hard as before. By withdrawing their effort, mavericks intend to prove that the manager does in fact need them.

The maverick believes that when the manager sees that things aren't going as well as they were, (prior to the withdrawal of the maverick's excessive effort), the manager will give the maverick more freedom to do things his way. This rarely happens as the manager is more likely to blame the maverick for things going wrong. The maverick will need to comply with the way that the manager wants the work completed or try to negotiate a different way. The maverick will probably have to assume all responsibility for possible failure, before the manager relinquishes his tight grip on his control. Mavericks will not do this if it seems that the risk of failure (possibly due to factors outside their control) is high, and the rewards are low and there is no way to address this balance. Mavericks aren't anyone's fool, and will not allow someone to shirk their responsibility or shoulder unacceptable or unrealistic risk onto them.

Mavericks will challenge even the simplest of tasks if they feel they are being managed rather than led, and they will not accept instructions that the rest of the workforce might find acceptable. They enjoy autonomy and have a strong need to be in control of their own destiny. They value their independence which is something that they will fight hard to maintain even if that leaves them at a disadvantage in the long term. Mavericks cannot help it, the need to be in control of themselves is innate and pressing.

This can cause some difficulty in the workplace, because their desire to be treated differently conflicts with most management styles that insist in treating all employees in the same way. This is not about treating mavericks like prima donnas, this is about changing your management or leadership style to get the best out of your talented employees and reducing the amount of management time you are using to deal with the consequences of not dealing with them uniquely.

The only way to satisfy the maverick's need for autonomy and the company's need for consistency is to employ a leadership style that is flexible enough to guide the maverick towards the desired outcome whilst allowing them to have a degree of autonomy that both parties can accept and value. This can be more difficult that it first seems as Extreme Mavericks (and those just beginning their path to becoming a Socialised Maverick) are either unaware of the effects they have on others, or don't care about them. Their preference for bluntness and the delivery of the unadulterated truth can be an uncomfortable experience for those on the receiving end. Often the temptation of their managers is to revert to managing them closely to bring them back into line. Resist this, unless you want your maverick to work against you not for you.

Define the success parameters

Compared to others, mavericks have unusually high self-esteem and confidence, which is why they prefer autonomy rather than strict rules that they will break any way. They are certain when they begin a task that they will complete it successfully. Mavericks do not expect to fail, unless they have calculated the likelihood of failure, and find it acceptable. If this is the case, they have factored the possibility of failure as a necessary step in self-knowledge or completion of the task. It is rare for mavericks to not consider the consequences of their actions, or non-action before the first step of the task has been undertaken.

For a task to be completed successfully the maverick needs to be certain that they will succeed before they begin. That search for certainty by the maverick, can manifest itself in many ways. Firstly, the maverick will ask lots of detailed questions before they begin or even consider beginning. The questions are likely to be very challenging, and can appear to be very diverse and at times off topic. It is often that mavericks are misunderstood at this stage, as the questions are misinterpreted as the maverick 'being difficult', rather than the search for certainty that it is. They want to know what they are being measured on and how will they know that they have not only completed the task, but that it has met all the stipulated criteria. In the questioning phase the maverick will elicit, the manager's hidden criteria and concerns so that all parties agree on exactly what must be achieved and in what timeframe.

One of the most common ways that mavericks elicit certainty is the maverick's insistence that they have access to you (their manager) whenever they need to check their understanding of an issue. This is their way of discovering what the success parameters are, and ensuring that nothing is 'lost in translation', which might happen if a third party was involved. Mavericks are great readers of body language, analysis, and good investigators, so they understand that their ability to get to the root of the issue will determine the project's success.

It is important that you give mavericks the amount of time that they might need to ensure they completely understand the task ahead and are certain that the task is within their capabilities. Do not be tempted to provide them with tasks that are not challenging, mavericks want to be stretched, and they will cause disruption if things slip into routine and become boring.

This can be a difficult balance to maintain and, in the early stages, mavericks can take up a lot of your time if you do not lead them properly. This is Pareto's Principle, the 80/20 Rule. Mavericks can take up 80% of your management time but be in the 20% of the company's top performers.

Give them recognition

> It was 7.30am and Jonathan and Jodie where in a cab on the way to the lawyers. Jonathan was a Director of the company and he asked Jodie why she was yawning so much.

Jodie: I'm just really tired, I've worked really long hours to help you prepare for taking over the other company. It's not something that someone in my role would normally do, but I've enjoyed the challenge. I've read all the relevant Employment and Commercial Law that pertains to this situation. I've done due diligence on the company, and outlined possible issues. I've consulted with the company's lawyers and designed new contracts, prepared a staff communication plan, a press release and numerous other tasks related to the takeover.

I've also managed to keep up with my existing work and running the department by working 20 hr days for weeks. I'm exhausted, and look forward to going back to a slower pace. It's been fun though.

Jonathan: *(glances at Jodie)* I'm tired too, I went to the theatre last night.

It was at that exact moment that Jodie realised that she would be handing in her resignation soon.

The most important thing to a maverick is recognition, whether that's recognition for their work or who they are. Ignoring them is guaranteed to ensure that they will participate in more and more activities that will force you to notice them and recognise them. This is truly a situation where if you do not recognise them for their expertise, you will recognise them for their capability to cause trouble.

Mavericks are wilfully independent and will fight for that independence at any given moment. Therefore, conventional management techniques, such as 'command and control' or 'carrot and stick' do not work and will cause more problems than they can solve.

Structure without structure

Mavericks prefer to work in an environment that supports 'structure without structure'. Without structure, mavericks find it difficult to start a task although it is important that the structure should not be constraining. One of the advantages about mavericks is that they can quickly see the holes in an argument or understand why a process isn't working properly. This is one of the key reasons why mavericks tend not to follow rules, they simply do not believe that the rules are helping the company achieve its stated goals. Therefore, it is important that managers check the reasoning as to why a maverick has stopped following a rule, rather than obsessing over a broken rule. It is important to ensure that there is a culture that supports openness and transparency. This enables the manager and the maverick to have a discussion on why the maverick was breaking the rules and what can be done to improve the processes.

Let them work to their own timetable

Whilst mavericks always meet their deadlines, they tend to work to their own timetable, preferring to create at times that suits them. This may be early morning or late at night. To achieve the best productivity out of a maverick, you should try to find ways to accommodate, even if that means they work at odd times during the day. Often, companies are nervous about allowing employees to work at times when the manager is not there, believing that the employee will not be productive unless they are supervised. This is probably because the manager is not very effective in his role. If the maverick respects and believes in you, then they will work tirelessly to ensure that your vision is implemented and is successful. They will do this in a way that can be unexpected at times. For example, they may insist on a company laptop so that they can work at 3 o'clock in the morning.

Need to feel trusted

Mavericks need to feel trusted to be able to reach peak performance. If a maverick perceives that they aren't trusted, they will not work at their peak capacity. In fact, it is probable that the Extreme Maverick will work actively against their manager. The maverick is highly influential and the manager may discover a groundswell of dissent from his other employees or his peers if they unfairly cross their maverick employee.

Give them boundaries

Mavericks need boundaries and they respect those that enforce them in the right way. Without boundaries, mavericks will keep pushing hoping that someone has the courage to get them to stop. Even Socialised Mavericks can become Extreme Mavericks by pushing on non-existent boundaries and it can become difficult to reign them in.

If you find yourself managing a maverick that is disengaged from the company or project in hand, so their behaviour has become unmanageable; give them a compelling reason to change. This will enable you to harness their creativity and insight for the benefit of the company.

6. Maverick Leaders

"Leadership is the activity of influencing people to cooperate toward some goal which they come to find desirable"

– Ordway Tead

Some individuals worry about having maverick leaders in their organisation. They feel that they are a threat to their authority, either because they are influential or that the maverick has more talent, or ability, than the leader has.

Good leaders should never be threatened by competence, there is much to be gained by encouraging Maverick Behaviourist traits in individuals. All companies benefit from the acceptance of maverick leaders who have their power harnessed effectively.

It is easy to dismiss the need for mavericks in the workplace and beyond, if you subscribe to the belief that mavericks are more trouble than they are worth. In fact, whilst being a maverick can bring innumerable rewards it can also rain down penalties of misunderstanding and disbelief. For Socialised Mavericks, this can make them very despondent and Extreme Mavericks very angry. Maverick Behaviourists may slip back to being Conformists and may never venture out as Behaviourists, which would be a terrible loss to the company.

Mavericks can be intimidating, either because of how they do something or because of the way that they are at ease with themselves. When you have high self-efficacy and self-esteem it can prove to be intimidating for those that do not enjoy such self-assurance. It can also make some believe that the maverick is just 'lucky', rather than acknowledge that the maverick has worked hard to develop the capabilities necessary for success and self-determination. Mavericks are very private people (something that extraverts work hard to hide!), so they do not disclose the amount of effort they put in to improve themselves or their knowledge base. This includes the type of 'touch points' that they are studying to improve their power bases.

Mavericks are the 'canaries in the coal mine', which means that due to their high sensitivity to adverse conditions, they can warn of a coming danger, many months in advance, of the absolute need to change direction in your activities or mindset. Therefore, mavericks are often considered to be visionary in their nature and explains why they are often many steps ahead of others. It is common for a maverick to know exactly how much time they have before others catch up with them. They have a great sense of timing and urgency.

I believe that if you can manage a maverick well, gain their respect and loyalty, then you are at the 'top of your leadership game'. The maverick will work hard to ensure your success, if they believe in you they make excellent number twos. If you have formal leadership authority over others and choose to manage the Conformists as if they were Maverick Behaviourists or mavericks, then you will become a highly influential and effective leader. If you have the skills and expertise to lead a maverick then you can lead anyone, anywhere, anytime.

Top performers

Mavericks are generally top performers since they prefer to become experts in their chosen field or specialism and they are always focused on the execution of the task and the output produced. They take pride in their work and would not knowingly miss a deadline or not complete a brief accurately. Mavericks tend to have good connections with influential people; which enables them to perform at a standard that exceeds the average person. They take their work seriously (or indeed any task they put their mind to) and expect those that they are working with to have the same work ethic. Mavericks will also seek to influence or manipulate key players in their team to produce the best output that they can, thus elevating the performance of the whole team.

Interestingly, Extreme Mavericks tend to be in the 20% of top performers within the organisation, even though they often cause 80% of the problems. Extreme Mavericks at work, which I have defined as Troublesome Talent®, can be very challenging. This is especially true if the management of the organisation is weak or ineffective and find it difficult to provide effective boundaries for the maverick. The problem with this Troublesome Talent®, is that because of their impressive talent, the management is reluctant to address the often-substantial fallout that can arise from them when they get upset or frustrated with others or the company. The management can get concerned about upsetting this maverick in case they become the subject of his ire and/or he ceases to perform in the manner of their liking.

Naturally influential, mavericks (of all types) will easily draw people towards them, that are prepared to follow their lead regardless of whether the maverick has actual formal authority for whatever it is that they are proposing.

Due to their ability to deliver good tangible results, mavericks tend to enjoy full autonomy, more leeway, and privileges than other employees can access. This can provide a lot of disruption and frustration within the workplace and if not managed properly, will quickly become divisive.

Subsequently, despite being top performers, mavericks (particularly Extreme Mavericks), can be very hard to manage, especially if you have an inflexible style of management. Mavericks expect to be managed differently from others and will not appreciate an autocratic style of management; or one where they have little influence. They expect to be recognised for their endeavours and rewarded fairly for them. Mavericks expect instant and open access to their leaders or managers and are resentful if this is not forthcoming. They will need a high level of autonomy to get their work done, preferring a delegating style of leadership (for example, Situational Leadership II, Blanchard) as a default. This style of leadership favours the leader being involved in only the decision, having delegated the responsibility and decision making process to the maverick. This style demonstrates that the leader has trust in the employee. It is essential that the maverick believes that he has your trust if he is going to work for you effectively, and with minimal disruption to you or the team.

Whilst Situational Leadership has been criticised for being inconsistent in its results, I feel that this inconsistency is probably due to the high need for leadership competence when applying this model accurately. The leader needs to have detailed knowledge of the task, ability, and motivation of the employee. Few managers/leaders have this capability and the ability to flex the model (e.g. change their leadership style to fit the task and the employee). It is, however, relatively easy for Socialised Mavericks to work and teach this model to others. This is due to their unique perception and deployment of their Maverick KEYSTONE Capabilities™.

The very worst way to manage a maverick is to micro manage them. Apart from the fact that this style of management is annoying and not usually necessary; it leads the maverick to believe that either you are a very insecure person (leading to a lack of trust and credibility), or that you do not trust them to do a good job. This lack of trust will make the maverick highly frustrated and resentful of you and the situation that they are in.

This will inevitably lead to the maverick disengaging and looking for distracting activities to keep him challenged or interested in remaining with the company or whilst looking for a new role. Dependant on the type of maverick this lack of engagement could become a very destructive distraction to others.

Therefore, a maverick will push hard for autonomy and will usually receive this, much to the disgust and annoyance of their colleagues. This will need to be addressed sensitively by the manager to reduce the potential 'fallout' of this decision. Many Conformists will feel that the maverick has been rewarded by being offered more favourable treatment. They will often believe that they have the same ability as the maverick and will overlook the substantial differentiators between them.

Mavericks will not accept poor performance from others or themselves

Mavericks are not comfortable with providing work that is of a poor standard and will work hard to ensure that they are never accused of sub-par performance. This is because poor performance causes significant cognitive dissonance as it is substantially contrary to how mavericks view themselves. They do not like feeling uncomfortable with their inner selves, so will work hard to be in a position where they can feel proud of their abilities. Subsequently, they tend to react badly when confronted with someone who is a poor performer, unless there is mitigating circumstances that does not point to laziness or a poor work ethic. They pride themselves with their own solid performance and expect others to care about their own performance as well. Mavericks find it hard to understand people who aren't ashamed to provide shoddy work; they see it as a serious character flaw.

The Socialised Maverick manager will immediately assess the ability of their employees as part of their assessment of the efficiency and general performance of the department. They will look for the weak links, the stars, and the average performers, and analyse where improvements can be made. This type of manager will sensitively share enough of this information with the employees for them to work together to bring substantial improvement.

This sensitivity remains true for the poor performer. The Socialised Maverick is extremely clear that they will not allow poor performance to be an accepted state for anyone in the department and will ensure that the poor performer is aware of this. After analysing the employee's ability, the maverick will decide if it's possible for the employee's performance to improve in an appropriate timescale. If it is, then they will work with the employee to ensure that improvement.

They will provide a clear structure, guidelines, and management overview for the employee to follow. The maverick will invest a considerable amount of time to enable the employee to be brought back in the fold. If personal issues are impacting the poor performance (and not ability), then they will be given space and understanding to get these things under control.

Whilst it is clear to the employee, that the Socialised Maverick will not tolerate under performance, their demeanour is one of support, care, encouragement and understanding. They are non-threatening or oppressive and the employee feels that the maverick is genuinely working with them to enable improvement; and this is often the case.

> Elizabeth was new to the company and had been observing Lisa's work ethic and rate and was not impressed. She knew that whilst Dennis had been Lisa's manager for a few years, he was not a competent manager. He had ability but had never received any management training. Dennis had not observed good management techniques from his previous manager (who Elizabeth had been brought in to replace).
>
> She noticed that Dennis could be a great manager but needed advice, training, and encouragement to get there. Elizabeth decided that Lisa would be a good starting place for Dennis to begin the learning he needed to become a great manager.
>
> She called Dennis into the office for a discussion.
>
> **Elizabeth:** Tell me about Lisa?
>
> **Dennis:** She's a lovely old lady, she's 60 and working until she decides to retire. Her work rate is slow, but everyone likes her and leaves her be. She will only be here another 5 years or so.

Elizabeth: *(sighs)* Your department is not meeting its objectives, in part because Lisa is not pulling her weight and you are ok with that?

Dennis: *(blusters)* Er, yes, no, I mean you've seen her, everyone goes to her for personal advice, she's lovely, it's like she is everyone's favourite mum or grandma. She just can't work fast and only really enjoys part of the role.

Elizabeth: Yes, I agree, I think she is lovely but I also think she is pulling the wool over your eyes.

Dennis: What do you mean?

Elizabeth: I've spent a lot of time with her on the department observing her work and listening to her explain to me what she does and how she does it.

What she lacks is proper systems and motivation. She is quite knowledgeable and no one seems to seek her advice on the work areas that sits in her expertise. She is in part underutilised in this area and over utilised in areas of admin that she doesn't enjoy and she's not good at.

Dennis: Oh, I didn't realise that.

Elizabeth: No, I know and you should have known that. You need to spend more time with your team understanding what they do and their strengths and weaknesses.

Dennis: Ok? Can you help?

Elizabeth: I'm glad you asked that *(she proceeded to explain to Dennis Lisa's strengths and weaknesses and where her expertise levels lie. She also gave examples of how Dennis' department could be re organised to work better which included a reorganisation of Lisa's work).*

Elizabeth agreed with Dennis a reasonable time to assess the situation for himself, to come up with a plan of implementation and communication that Elizabeth could agree with. After a few tweaks by Elizabeth, Dennis proceeded to implement his proposed changes.

Elizabeth: How's it going Dennis?

Dennis: Good, the department's running better and I've taken admin away from Lisa and have expanded her role around her expertise.

I can see that she's good at it, but she's just too slow. It's now really obvious that she has such a negative impact on the department due to her work rate, I can't believe I didn't notice it before. Do you think we should sack her?

Elizabeth: *(She smiled, marvelling at just how far he had come in recognising his responsibilities and his tolerance of poor performance, in such a short time).* No I don't. Whilst you have changed her work into something she loves doing, you've not attempted to change her attitude. She's not stupid, far from it. You have, however, let her and the whole company believe that she can provide poor performance due to her age and that you require little from her.

Elizabeth took some time to advise Dennis on how he could increase Lisa's performance and how to encourage and motivate her. At their next meeting, Dennis could report that Lisa's performance was extremely good and she was now an essential part of the department. He had also initiated a similar system with the rest of his employees and could state that not only was the whole department's performance increased, but morale had as well.

This is an ideal situation that benefits the company and its employees. If Elizabeth had been an Extreme Maverick, the results and solution would likely have been quite different:

Elizabeth: Dennis, what are you doing about Lisa? She's not pulling her weight, she must go

Dennis: But she's a lovely lady and has worked here many years

Elizabeth: I don't care, she's making me look bad and isn't really adding anything to the department

Dennis: So you want me to just sack her? Have you spent any time with her?

Elizabeth: Why should I? You are her boss not me. Just get rid of her and let me know when's it done so we can recruit someone else.

Extreme Mavericks' tolerance for poor performers is particularly low, especially if their poor performance is negatively affecting the maverick, either in reputation or more tangibly on their possible chance for success. They have no problems jettisoning others to ensure that their own record of achievement or perceived reputation doesn't suffer.

There is little difference to their attitude if the maverick is a colleague or a poor performer, rather than an employee that they are responsible for. Extreme Mavericks will work hard to remove the poor performer from the team and by contrast, Socialised Mavericks will look for ways to support or encourage. The Extreme Maverick will openly challenge the manager as they lose respect in them, which can be quite demoralising for the manager as well as disturbing to the team.

However, if the Socialised Maverick believes that the poor performance is due to a lazy attitude or incapability they would push hard for something to be done about it (up to and including the dismissal of the employee).

If the maverick's manager ultimately accepts poor performance this will demotivate the Socialised Maverick who will cease to perform well and the Extreme Maverick will seek to find challenge in rectifying their manager's decision.

Mavericks break the rules often and that's a good thing!

One of the things about mavericks that people simultaneously love and hate is their propensity to break the rules and get away with it. We've discussed earlier that this is due to their maverick attributes working in unison, especially their wilful intention, honest belief, execution and output and success driven attributes.

It is not surprising to realise that different types of mavericks will break the rules for different reasons. Socialised Mavericks will break the rules because they can see that the current rules are unhelpful and are not working effectively. They will try to change the rules to increase the potential for success. They will aim to reason, negotiate or influence and if that is not working, will aim to subvert the system in a way that can be justified. Whilst Extreme Mavericks will break the rules for the same reason, however, they will not care if the solution that they implement can be justified. They will also be more likely to break the rules because they are bored and need a challenge.

Mavericks realise that those that are successful are generally forgiven much. They also believe that in most circumstances it is easier to seek forgiveness rather than permission. Therefore, they will proceed with their endeavours as if they had permission. Therefore, breaking the rules to gain bigger and more sustainable success and progress in the task.

If in the Socialised Maverick's assessment, it appears that it is just not possible to influence a change of the rules, and to subvert them is too high a personal risk, they will switch tactics. They will carry on as the process is designed, but this time they will put their impressive resources towards assessing and detailing the consequences of following the rules. For example, they will provide an analysis that shows the opportunity cost of the status quo, the financial implications as well as the cost of disengagement, inefficiency, and the effect on customers.

Once they have collated and assessed the data, turned it into a format that the organisation will accept, they will present it as an argument for change. If, even after this, the company chooses to ignore the excellent argument for change the Socialised Maverick will begin to look outside the organisation for a better working environment. It is also likely that they will become despondent and disengaged (mavericks dislike doing anything that they know will ultimately lead to failure, especially as they see it as a personal affront to their sensibilities), which will eventually have a ripple effect throughout the organisation.

Extreme Mavericks have less patience than Socialised Mavericks when it comes to implementing the need for change. Their idea of influence is to announce that the current system isn't working and they have a new and better system that needs implementing right away. They are most likely to be right, but do not believe in the need to get people to 'buy into' the change that's needed. They can be extremely charming and will attempt to influence in this way, moving onto brute force and manipulation if this doesn't work immediately. If the organisation cannot see 'the error of their ways', the maverick will just carry on as if the change had been agreed, and challenge anyone who has the mettle to dispute otherwise.

The difference between the two types of maverick at this point is that the Socialised Maverick will seek cooperation and be cogent of others feelings when they break the rules. They will seek to minimise dissent and will look for opportunities for buy in from others. Alternatively, Extreme Mavericks feel that 'you had your chance,' and will not be looking for ways to minimise dissent. He will look for ways to 'rub your nose in it', so that he can demonstrate just how right he was in the first place.

Another reason mavericks may have for breaking the rules is that they are bored and could do with the challenge. They may be genuinely interested in what may happen once the rule has been broken, or they may be trying to antagonise someone by deliberating refusing to comply with the rules. They may be testing a hypothesis on a person or environment and is interested in the possible outcome of their experimentation. Mavericks have complex personalities and thinking processes.

There is always a reason for mavericks to break the rules and with a little discernment you will be able to ascertain the reason and take steps to address the situation. (This may mean that you should change the rules because the maverick has highlighted a flaw in your systems and his solution is the better one to take).

> Rachel had just joined the company as a senior manager and was aware that she had taken over a department that had a poor reputation. The department was thought to be knowledgeable but inefficient, able to function well but lacked empathy and dynamism.
>
> Following her 'temperature check', she could tell that the department was lack lustre in its output and temperament. They had little empathy for the managers that they supported and were quick to point out management error and just as quick to dismiss their own inadequacies. A lot of time was wasted through idle gossip and they had little pride in the quality of their own output. They had the worst case of Ivory Tower complex she had ever seen.
>
> Rachel had two managers working under her (who were acting like glorified employees, not managers) and she knew if the performance of the employees were to

improve she needed to change the managers' attitudes. The managers were not used to being challenged and were keen to maintain the status quo.

Rachel knew that she needed to get the managers excited in their work again and to have pride in the results and the impact that they could have. She knew that this problem was multifaceted and that a solution would take some time to be fully implemented.

As a team, they had worked out what they were currently doing as opposed to what they should be doing. The conclusion was that some of the priorities were mixed up and there were activities that they should stop doing and some that they should start doing.

It was clear that the status quo was not benefitting the company nor the department. The managers did not believe that they had the power to change anything, especially as the company's expectations of the department had not changed in years.

One of the things that Rachel decided to do, was to ask the managers to redesign their respective areas of responsibilities (including the structure of the department and the employees' workload/responsibilities) to ensure that they could provide the right output (in quality as well as quantity). Their brief included the statement that what they propose must make a difference and that they should be proud of the result.

Rachel knew that whatever the department came up with would be a hard sell to the rest of the company. She knew that what the company really needed to do, to ensure that it met its stated goals, would require her department to expand its responsibilities and to let go some of the tasks that it was doing in favour of returning them to the other departments. This would be cause for concern due to the lack of expertise in the other departments. It would require a staged release of responsibility and training to ensure that nothing fell between the cracks.

When the managers had finished their proposals, Rachel sat down with them to work out what was feasible and what timescales would be needed. She noticed just how much their morale had increased and how innovative some of their proposals were. The managers just needed to be released from the constraints of the culture and the status quo to be effective. They needed to feel trusted and believed in, which would be a relatively new experience for them.

It was clear that for the department to really 'sing' a complete restructure would be needed. Without prior authorisation from the Director, Rachel and her managers set to work. They worked out a complete restructuring plan, including a change of responsibilities within and externally to the department. This included implementation and training plans for the managers of the other departments who would be taking on new responsibilities.

Rachel worked out a cost analysis for the change and an opportunity cost for not implementing the change. With this information, she went to the Director with her proposal.

Whilst the Director could see the justification for change he was alarmed. The proposed changes would centralise a lot of responsibility and power into Rachel's department and he was suspicious of her motives. She had only been in the department for a month and it seemed that she was making an impressive grab for power. He was not convinced that he wanted to change the status quo that was working before, albeit imperfectly. Nor did he want to give the other departments more work as he knew that there would be a lot of resistance and resentment from them. The Director told Rachel that he would not approve the changes and he wanted her to carry on with the way that the previous manager had run the department.

Whilst Rachel was annoyed by his lack of foresight, careful questioning outlined his real concerns. She decided that the changes were essential and therefore should take place anyway.

Rachel made the department changes that were necessary, explaining to her managers and employees, that they were implementing a two-step process. It was imperative that the department structural changes were kept within the department and not communicated to the rest of the company. She trained the managers and employees on their new responsibilities and began producing reports based on the new efficiencies. These reports provided essential company data that allowed the company to be run more efficiently and allowed her department to 'add more value'. The data was not complete however, as it required the external structural changes that she had suggested to be implemented.

A couple of months later the Director asked to see her. He wanted to know what had brought about the efficiency, dynamism, and usefulness of her department. At this point she provided him with an amended proposal that would fully implement the changes that she had previously suggested.

The Director smiled, it was a 'no brainer', Rachel could demonstrate the need for change and how she would implement such a change. Once the change had been fully implemented, it triggered a wide-reaching change of activities across the company. Ultimately, this change was beneficial for the company and shattering the status quo was the best thing that could have taken place.

Socialised Mavericks tend to break the rules because they see themselves as catalysts for change. They have a 'hawk's eye' vision of what needs to change and the dogged determination to make it happen.

Mavericks work at an intense pace

Mavericks expect everyone to work at the same pace as they do and find it very difficult to work with anyone that they believe is slacking or not pulling their weight. Because they are execution and output driven they have no problem with working long hours to ensure that the work is completed satisfactorily. They cannot understand why others would not want to do the same. They believe that if an employee is not happy in their job they should leave, after all that is something that they would do. Maverick managers need to be very careful that they do not overwork their employees because they assume that they will have a similar work pace to them. Mavericks tend to think quickly and due to their planning abilities, are often considering possibilities and outcomes several steps ahead, and wrongly assume others are doing the same.

This can mean that they can stop an activity that a member of their staff is completing and switch tack and ask them to do something else because the maverick can foresee that it isn't going to work or that there is a better way for a goal to be completed. This can be very disconcerting or frustrating because the reason for the change is not always apparent, because the maverick is working several steps ahead. The maverick will often forget to provide their reasoning, because for them the reason is obvious and they expect everyone else to know the reason as well. This can breed discontentment because it can look like the maverick does not appreciate the work that the employee is doing or worse still is unsure of what they (the maverick) are doing. The maverick becomes upset because he doubts the employee's ability as he wonders why the employee did not realise that their endeavour wasn't going to work and change their tack and do something with a higher probability for success. He forgets that Conformists will tend to follow the path that they have been set unless actively encouraged to question everything and to stand up to what they believe in. Good maverick leaders provide this encouragement on a regular basis. Maverick leaders attempt to change all Conformists to Maverick Behaviourists.

Mavericks can often get quite impatient of those that can't keep up and if not careful can communicate this impatience most effectively. For example, they may become snappy or derisive of the other employees; especially if they think that they are carrying them. They can also show their discontentment in their body language. Extreme Mavericks are likely to take out their frustrations on others and bully them into picking up their pace. They are also likely to discredit them by telling others that the 'slow working' employee is lazy or incapable of doing the work and is affecting the team.

Socialised Mavericks are more likely to take time to discover why an employee is not keeping up and work with them to implement changes. They will also recognise if they, the Socialised Maverick, is being unreasonable in expecting the work rate of others to increase. In any effect, their first thoughts would be to seek to influence others to change. It is likely that they will be successful, if they are not, their thoughts are most likely to turn to how they can remove this employee from the team. This may seem like a harsh conclusion to their impatience. It is not, because you need to remember that a Socialised Maverick is always fair and objective. They will have tried other alternatives and would have considered their own motives in the situation. If they can't influence reasonable change in the employee, then it's likely to be a hopeless case and it is better for the organisation that the employee and it part company.

The only exception to the Socialised Maverick's reasonableness is when they are under extreme stress. This is when their Extreme Maverick tendencies are likely to slip out. For example, they may say hurtful things to others and may act in a manipulative way. It is times like this that they can damage relationships beyond repair, often because the other person is left wondering whether the maverick always thought these things but just didn't say them. It is unlikely that this possibility is true, it is more probable that the Socialised Maverick is hurting and is therefore lashing out at others in the most effective way that they can (quickly assessing vulnerabilities and exploiting them). This type of behaviour will always be a surprise to others as they would not have previously considered the Socialised Maverick to be capable of this type of behaviour.

Once the crisis is over the Socialised Maverick will feel quite remorseful and will work hard to repair relationships and communicate, where they can, the reason for their atypical behaviour. If they are not forgiven the Socialised Maverick will reconsider their position because they will wonder why their extensive 'good behaviour', is not enough to offset their extremely rare 'bad behaviour'. They could become very despondent and wonder why they are working in an organisation that will not forgive such atypical behaviour and yet forgives very bad transgressions from others who have a poorer work ethic or ability on a regular basis.

There are many reasons for this lack of acceptance, one of the most prevalent is that the Socialised Maverick may have shocked others and not fit the stereotype, or expectations that others might have been expecting of them. Another may be that their success has caused some jealously from their colleagues in the past, and their recent behaviour may have taken some 'shine from their halo', and the jealous colleagues want to exploit the opportunity.

Finally, mavericks can burn themselves out by fulfilling their need to exceed others expectations of them, and their internal need to hit a deadline. If necessary, they will complete other's work and increase their own hours to ensure that the work is completed. Mavericks hate missing deadlines. Socialised Mavericks and Maverick Behaviourists are likely to keep their increased work load and anti-social hours to themselves as they are focusing on getting the work done, rather than receiving some sort of accolade on how they got the work done.

Lawrence had been working at the small company (approximately 200 employees) for three months now. His expertise was respected by others, and he was highly thought of by the workforce, his employees, and the Directors. Lawrence loved his job and the challenge that it brought. He was enabling the company to radically change their status quo (internally and in the marketplace) and he loved the successes that this brought the company. He believed in the company and wanted to help make the Directors successful.

Lawrence had explained to the Directors that his department was understaffed but they were unwilling to sanction additional employees. Lawrence's reaction was to continue to change what and how his department worked. This would show its potential and justify the need for more staff.

His workload was increasing, seemingly exponentially, and the only way Lawrence could cope was to increase his own hours to match. For three months, he did this despite his peers taking long lunches, early finishes, and a seemingly lacklustre approach. He loved his work and wanted to see the Directors (who personally owned the company) become more successful.

One day Lawrence met a girl on the way to work and exchanged numbers with her. After a while it seemed that they might develop a relationship beyond phone calls and emails and they both decided that it might be nice if they met up. As luck would have it, they discovered that whilst they lived quite far from each other, they did work close to each other and could meet up at lunch times to get to know each other better. For two blissful weeks

Lawrence and his girlfriend met up every lunchtime to spend time together. It made his long work hours more bearable.

After the two weeks, Lawrence's manager (one of the Directors) ask to meet him to discuss his work.

Andrea: How's it going Lawrence?

Lawrence: Great! *(He proceeded to outline several recent successes and things he was working on)*

Andrea: Ok, so you are happy working here then?

Lawrence: Yes, why are you asking?

Andrea: Well, the MD asked me to check as you don't seem as committed as you once were

Lawrence: Huh? *(Lawrence thought of the extremely long hours that he was working and his successes. He was honestly perplexed, he knew that neither his work quality or work output could be questioned. His work was of a high standard and exceeded not only his peers but the Directors also).* What do you mean?

Andrea: *(Not meeting his eyes).* Well he's noticed that for the last two weeks you have been having a lunch break, you haven't been doing that before. He's questioning your commitment to the company.

Lawrence: I'm sorry? *(Holding his anger in),* he is questioning my commitment to the company, despite me producing more innovative work of better quality than other people? I work longer hours than anyone, Directors included and I'm understaffed by at least two employees. Despite that, the department has made significant changes that benefits the company immensely, including the bottom line and the workload of my department has gone up fourfold!

He is upset that I'm now taking a lunch break that I'm legally entitled to? When my peers and Directors regularly take 3 plus hours for lunch every day? Are you kidding me? Do *you* have any complaints about my work or attitude?

Andrea: No, I don't. You do an amazing job and we are very lucky to have you working for us. Shall I tell the MD that you are committed to your job?

Lawrence: *(Unable to maintain eye contact).* Yes

Back at his desk, Lawrence reviewed the conversation. He was absolutely flabbergasted. Lawrence was waking up in the morning at 3am and working at home on the work laptop until 6am. He then got ready and went to work reaching his desk for 7.30 am having grabbed a breakfast wrap on the way in. He normally (last two weeks excepted) worked through lunch and left the office around 6pm. Once home he had dinner and then switched the work lap top on at 10pm working through until 12am. Ready to get up for 3am to start his work day again.

He did this Monday to Friday. He switched on his work laptop on a Sunday evening around 8pm, working until around 10pm. He didn't have a life, all he did was work, for what now seemed to be an unappreciative company. He thought he was valued but he was wrong.

He pondered deeply on this and realised that he was burning himself out for negligible gain. Not only was he not experiencing a personal life, but the only thing his company was focusing on was the fact that he was taking his legally sanctioned lunch break. The Directors knew he was working strange hours, having received emails timestamped in the early hours of the morning, but he realised that despite all the good work that he was doing they did not appreciate him nor cared about his welfare.

He realised that things must change and he started working on a plan to reduce his cognitive dissonance. The change would, no doubt, be very noticeable.

There are many facets to the above example, that serve to highlight the lengths that a Socialised Maverick will go to, to ensure that a task is completed. Including the fact that their motives are often misunderstood. In this example, Lawrence was working excessive hours for the company to help save them money, (by not hiring the much-needed employees), and to complete their stated mission and vision statement. He enjoyed his job and truly believed in the company. He did not consider letting the company know how much hours he was working (before the meeting) because he had willingly concluded that this was the price he was prepared to pay to ensure that the work was completed and his work performance remained high. He didn't feel that it made much point complaining about something that he had chosen to do. Lawrence did not complain during the meeting because he felt that it did not provide an advantage to do so. It would have not made any difference to the Director's mindset, after all the MD thought it was perfectly acceptable for someone not to have a lunch break every day whilst the rest of the company took excessive ones. Lawrence felt stupid for not having seen earlier that he was being used by the company and taken advantage of. He had willingly put himself on the path to burn out for no appreciative reason. This is something that he needed to rectify and if he complained now, then he would be alerting the company that he was unhappy with their intervention. This would take the advantage of surprise from him.

Mavericks are catalysts for change

Whenever mavericks are tasked to do anything they will assess and analyse whether there is a need to change the status quo first. If they sense that there is a need to do so they will not shy away from trying to influence or manipulate a change. Mavericks being natural leaders, expect others to follow them and be keen to help them succeed in implementing something that might ultimately destroy the comfortable status quo.

Mavericks are often hired to be the catalyst of change in the organisation having already impressed on the company their ability to make a difference. Unlike most individuals, mavericks can give an accurate indication on how long it would take to implement change and will consider all aspects of the change. From the practical aspects to the communication of the change and how to influence others to accept the change easily, to the training and feelings of others.

Mavericks are unconcerned on whether they have formal authority to suggest or implement change as they are often focused on meeting the stated goal or fulfilling their responsibilities. They are not interested in other people's fears or egos. They are also aware that other people want to please the maverick or watch what they do, before deciding their own cause of action.

For example, if you watch either the British or American X Factor programme, you will notice that the artists may receive positive accolades from the judges but they do not begin their celebration until Simon Cowell (a maverick) speaks. If he pronounces the act as 'good', they are ecstatic. If Simon says he didn't like the act, his pronouncement takes a definite shine off their celebrations and they are bitterly disappointed. To the performer, it's the maverick's opinion that counts the most.

Maverick leadership

Leadership is one of those funny, fuzzy concepts where everyone can point to a good or bad leader and yet struggle to define exactly what leadership **is**. Leadership for many has become a job title where the holder has little authority or autonomy and is really a manager of tasks and people; rather than someone that can inspire, motivate and influence others to achieve a goal or vision.

Many leadership models concentrate on the execution of a task and the management of the people, bypassing the character traits of the leader and how these characteristics influence the ability of the team/individual to achieve goals. They can also presuppose that leadership is something that happens to people in an organisational context rather than the fact that a true leader is someone who leads through all aspects of their lives not just when they are at work.

You can recognise a leader wherever they are, whatever they are doing. Even introverted leaders have presence.

Perhaps the aim of an organisation should be to ensure that all employees can become Maverick Behaviourists and thus transform the company's ability to thrive. These Maverick Behaviourists would join Socialised Mavericks in becoming maverick leaders. This transformation is not concerned with awarding job titles and increasing wages. This is about an individual having the autonomy to do the right thing and making a difference to the organisation. This is about having engaged employees and inspiring effective leaders. Providing responsibility to the employees and being comfortable with the results!

The employee's aim to self-improvement (especially in the workplace), should be to become either a Maverick Behaviourist or a Socialised Maverick. Individuals who wish to influence others (either formally or informally) should use the Maverick DRIVEN Leadership™ methodology; being cogent of maverick power and capabilities. This will, therefore, transform their existence not just at work but at home too.

This would of course, call for a different type of leader, a different expectation from the norm.

Organisations are filled with managers who are not happy when they see natural leaders emerging from within their workforce. Especially if the environment typically supports Conformists and bureaucratical leaders, rather than free thinking employees (mavericks) that would like to challenge the status quo.

Leadership style is the manner and approach of providing direction, implementing plans, and motivating people. As seen by the employees, it includes the total pattern of explicit and implicit actions performed by their leader (Newstrom, Davis, 1993). Leadership style is something that individuals use to define a leader. It is not enough to tell someone something, they will judge you by what you do as well.

Socialised and Extreme Mavericks tend to use different leadership styles, which can appear similar in outcome, even though they differ wildly in maverick intent. Extreme Mavericks favour a highly charismatic leadership style, whereas Socialised Mavericks prefer a transformational leadership style. Both types of leadership styles inspire and motivate their team members, but their focus is different. Transformational leaders, transform their teams and their organisations (or environment), and charismatic leaders are more concerned with themselves and ensuring that their situation and environment suits their purposes. They may not want to change anything and may resist, any suggestion of change.

Extreme Maverick's Leadership style – Charismatic in nature

Charismatic leaders encourage certain behaviours by dint of their powerful personality, ability to persuade and their eloquent communication. Whilst their communication may not be objectively eloquent it is perfect for their preferred audience (think President Trump during his election campaign). It depends on their values and morality whether the charismatic leader is positive or negative in their influence.

The Extreme Maverick is a master of body language and is driven by his wilful intention and honest belief. He can use referent, expert, and coercive power effectively. He connects well with people (normally on a deep emotional level) on first meeting, he is charming and whilst you are talking to him you believe that you are very important to him. He is encouraging and makes you feel special and appreciated.

It is important to remember that this type of leader will change his rhetoric depending on the audience he is with at any given time. The Extreme Maverick will use emotional arguments especially if he is challenged on his logic and cannot win. Being charming, for him, is just another form of (emotional) manipulation, and therefore often eclipses rational arguments.

This type of maverick is not concerned with changing the status quo, unless it is to his advantage. He has a need to be listened to and worshipped, and can rapidly become either a situational narcissist or psychotic narcissist. He does not accept challenge easily and can be quick to discredit others if it means he gets ahead.

Charismatic leaders tend to be more concerned with themselves than other people, although you may need to pay rapt attention to notice this. They tend to form a tight group of followers around them, who are totally aligned to the Extreme Maverick. To be part of the group is to be a projection of the Extreme Maverick. You come under his protection and believe everything he says.

Once he has his group, he will start to distinguish between 'us and them', ensuring that his group are aware that they are superior to others. With a huge ego and self-efficacy, the Extreme Maverick will often ignore warnings to cease their behaviour. This is because most people will not give him a compelling reason to change. The inherent danger with charismatic leaders is that they begin to need the adoration that they are subjected to and become a situational narcissist, intolerant of challenge and changing their behaviour to one that they believe merits worship or infallibility from their audience.

Socialised Maverick's Leadership style – Transformational in nature

There are many similarities between charismatic and transformational leadership. The key difference is the focus of the leader and his intention. Socialised Mavericks have no need to be adored or worshiped, they lead because they want to transform the status quo. They want to develop their followers, and empower them to become Maverick Behaviourists.

They also present a clear vision to inspire and encourage others to achieve. Extreme Mavericks tend not to waste their time inspiring others as they use the power of their personality to enforce change.

Socialised Mavericks, like Extreme Mavericks can also have a charismatic style, be influential and engaging with others. However, they work with or for their followers rather than rearranging things solely for their own benefit. Socialised Mavericks see this rearrangement as unethical. They understand that they are role models and that their followers emulate them.

Maverick DRIVEN Leadership™

Maverick leaders, regardless of whether they have formal or informal authority all utilise, what I am calling, the Maverick DRIVEN Leadership™ methodology at the heart of what they do. This leadership methodology provides a foundation for success, and thus the credibility of the leader. Successful mavericks and Maverick Behaviourists use this methodology naturally and it's this authenticity that enables people to follow them.

Aspiring leaders can also use the Maverick DRIVEN Leadership™ Methodology to improve their leadership ability. My intention for this book is not to provide a fully detailed description and explanation of my Maverick DRIVEN Leadership™ Methodology just a brief overview to whet the appetite:

- **D**etermination
- **R**eputation
- **I**nfluence
- **V**ersatility
- **E**xecution
- **N**arration

D is for determination

All good leaders have a healthy dose of determination, the will to succeed. Determination allows us to prioritise what is important; it can enable us to use failure to inform success, and meet our commitment to others. Mavericks are output and execution driven and have a rock solid wilful intention which help fuel their dogged determination. They will keep going until they achieve the objective that they have set themselves.

Once mavericks have settled onto an objective they can be narrowly focused on its achievement and this can cause disruption, and where other people are concerned disharmony. This is because mavericks will take shortcuts to achieve their objectives and will ride roughshod over others and their feelings.

The determination of the maverick can be harnessed by discovering what their objective is and to ensure that is aligned to the company's objectives. Spending time with your maverick to find out what rules will likely to hinder him will enable you to decide what steps need to be taken.

R is for reputation

Socialised Mavericks pride themselves on their ability to garner trust and their excellent reputation for integrity and competence. They will lend the project (or person) their reputation to give it a better chance for success.

Socialised Mavericks see their associates or employees as a projection of themselves, so will insist that these individuals have a good reputation. How they do is a reflection on the Socialised Maverick's ability to lead them well. This is one of the reasons why this type of maverick ensures that there is trust between them and their associates and that their associates can fulfil their tasks in a manner that is acceptable to the maverick.

Maverick leaders are known for their competence, their ability to get things done efficiently and well. Their reputation for success enables others to trust their leadership, even when the pathway does not seem clear to them. They believe that the maverick knows what they are doing and where they are going.

I is for influence

All leaders use their influence to persuade their followers to cooperate with them and enable their followers to execute the leader's wishes. Maverick leaders take for granted their capability to lead due to their ability to understand people and the dynamics of influence and persuasion.

Mavericks rely on their personal influence rather than their positional influence. They are highly influential people although when they are not lead properly this influence tends to become manipulation.

V is for versatility

Good leaders are versatile in their approach, thinking and in their implementation. Mavericks can take this to the extreme and are often versatile when it comes to bending rules, cutting corners, and understanding boundaries. When linked with their high determination in achieving their goals they can cause havoc in an organisation that has poor leadership.

Mavericks are nothing but flexible and despise others who persist in becoming fixed to a certain dogma without review or adjustment to changing circumstances. They often use resources unexpectedly and in different contexts than what they were designed or envisioned to be used for. Mavericks are creative when it comes to designing and implementing new solutions which is one of the reasons they enjoy a high level of success.

E is for execution

A key capability of mavericks is their output and execution driver, which means they do not believe that anything can be classified as a success if it has not been executed well.

This is one of the reasons why they tend to have a strong reputation and track record of competence. All mavericks guarantee that their tasks are executed in a manner that they anticipated and defined before the start of the project. They ensure that their followers have a similar execution mindset and never get so wrapped up in the idea that they forget the necessity of completion.

N is for narration

A key component to the maverick's ability to influence is their talent for storytelling. They can weave compelling stories that draw their followers to their vision or encourage them to take risks that they hadn't expected to take.

Good maverick leaders also provide a narrative as to what is happening, as it's happening. This allows them to translate and pace actual events, enabling them to influence the actions of their followers.

This influence increases participation through encouragement and explanation and referencing to the vision and the need for change. This narration facilitates a highly-engaged leadership style where the employee or follower feels inspired and protected by the leader. The leader creates a 'circle of safety' (Simon Sinek), for his followers that is returned by their loyalty and trust.

John Maxwell stated that leadership is influence nothing more, nothing less. I agree that without influence you cannot lead. Influence is formed from many sub concepts and that the secret behind maverick leaders is that they understand that leadership is a relationship of trust.

This includes its key components of integrity and competence. The Maverick KEYSTONE Capabilities™, maverick attributes and effective use of power are all ingredients to the secret recipe of maverick success.

Epilogue

HR: We are going to have to discipline John. This can't go on, he's upset Janey again and I'm fed up of having her crying in my office day after day.

This is bullying and it has to stop. What are you going to do about it?

Manager: Look I know that John can be insensitive at times, but he means well. It's just that he doesn't suffer fools gladly and Janey's work has been slipping ...

HR: That's no excuse ...

Manager: I know, I know... what am I going to do though? The customer loves him and the Sales Director thinks he's wonderful. You do know that he has outsold everyone in the company, every year for the last 4 years? I can't discipline him just because he makes someone cry occasionally. What would I do if he leaves?

HR: So, what are you suggesting?

Whilst the above conversation is commonplace in companies, the solution itself isn't always forthcoming. The right intervention for John can only take place after a fulsome conversation between the HR Manager and John's manager; taken within the context of understanding John and his current work performance. The managers should consider where John is on © Maverick Continuum™ to see how it impacts his behaviour and performance.

The managers will need to work together if they wish to resolve the behavioural issue that John is presenting, and decide (amongst other things) whether there is a basis of truth that is fuelling his actions. For example, is Janey a poor performer not managed properly? Is John really a bully, or a peak performer frustrated at the lack of commitment from Janey? Is Janey manipulating the situation and using tears to hide the fact that she isn't performing?

Maverick leaders understand that context is everything.

John's behaviour warrants maverick analysis

If the managers want to address the situation properly then they cannot jump to conclusions and assume that Janey is a victim and John is the aggressor. It is important to come to the right conclusion, as the results could have far reaching consequences.

Janey's behaviour and performance, therefore, will need to be assessed using effective management techniques that will bring clarity to the situation. Regardless of Janey's assessment, John's behaviour still warrants a maverick analysis.

When conducting John's analysis, his manager needs to take into consideration the following:

- What exactly is driving John's behaviour, what influence does his maverick attributes play?

- What impact is John's personality having on his behaviour? (consider each one of the Big 5 Personality traits).

- Where is John on the Maverick Continuum™, what impact does this have?

- What is the effect of John's maverick mindset?

- How effectively is John using his Maverick KEYSTONE Capabilities™?

- In what way is John harnessing his maverick power? Is there a need for an intervention here?

- What type of maverick leader is John?

- How well is John's manager utilising the Maverick DRIVEN Leadership™ methodology?

Following this analysis, the manager will be better placed to answer the HR Manager, and implement a solution that improves both employees' behaviour and performance and impacts positively on and within the organisation.

The secret power behind successful (maverick) leaders

Maverick leaders are courageous people who do not wait for formal authority to lead. They lead with integrity and trust and are role models that people want to emulate.

They challenge the status quo because their unique perspective enables them to see clearly what needs to change to bring success to theirs (and yours) endeavours. Working with maverick leaders may be challenging but it is fun and purposeful. Translating a clear (revolutionary) vision into evolutionary steps, they bring meaningful purpose to what they do and a reputation that you enjoy basking in.

The secret power behind successful leaders can be expressed by understanding and utilising the KP MAP acronym:

KEYSTONE capabilities
Power (Maverick)

Maverick Mindset
Attributes (Maverick)
Personality (Maverick)

Maverick leaders are on the winning team, and have a level of self-confidence and inner peace that is envied by others. The question to ask yourself is:

Is this you? If not do you want it to be?

Find out where you are on the © Maverick Continuum™, and begin your journey from Conformist to Maverick Behaviourist or Extreme Maverick to Socialised Maverick.

If you have been judged to be a Socialised Maverick, begin your journey to mastery. Remember, mavericks challenge all things, all the time. This includes your own development.

Successful leaders are maverick leaders (Socialised Mavericks or Maverick Behaviourists).

Within this book, you have learnt the key things that you need to become a successful leader, and how to inspire others around you to do the same. There is now a deeper understanding of why Socialised Mavericks present the best model of leadership and why the toxicity of Extreme Mavericks don't.

I have provided you with information on how to analyse, understand and influence the mavericks that you come across. If you have maverick behaviour, then you are able to understand yourself better, and improve the impact that you are currently making. As you begin to master your own personal maverick journey, you will also be able to recognise and understand Extreme Mavericks and their controlling tactics. This should mean that you will be less likely to be manipulated by Extreme Mavericks and less willing to let them have free access to what they want, when they want it, how they want it.

Harnessing the secret power of successful leaders (including your own power), should be demonstratively easier, having understood KP MAP (the maverick capabilities, power utilisation, mindset, attributes, personality) and the Maverick DRIVEN Leadership™ methodology.

As an aspiring successful maverick leader, take back control, and become truly powerful.

Follow me on the path to mastery ...

About the Author

Judith Germain is a hopeful pragmatist that believes that one day we will live in a world where the truly powerful strives for the greater good. Where every person is a maverick leader, inspired to do the right thing, regardless of the consequences.

A world where character and integrity has a higher premium than personality and bureaucracy. This will be transformational for the organisations that they work for and the people that they meet.

A Fellow of the Chartered Institute of Personnel and Development, and MBA (PgDip) graduate, Judith is a trained Executive Coach and senior HR/Operations consultant.

For over 20 years, she has worked with hundreds of leaders to nurture, develop, and inspire them to become successful leaders that can be trusted. To be maverick leaders that can effectively and ethically influence others; to challenge the status quo to create sustainable successful results.

Judith is the leading authority on mavericks and maverick leadership. She is also a keynote speaker and co-author of Amazon bestseller *BusinessWise*. Her expert opinion has appeared in numerous publications including national broadsheets and leading industry press.

A brief note from the author

Additional information and resources are available from the sources below:

> A free bonus article **Maverick leader: Nature or Nurture?** at: www.maverickparadox.com/books
>
> Information on mavericks, successful leadership and how to hire Judith at: www.maverickparadox.com
>
> Information on Judith's forthcoming books at: www.maverickparadoxbooks.com

Thank you for taking the time to read my book. If you enjoyed **The Maverick Paradox: The secret power behind successful leaders**, I would be grateful if you would leave a review on Amazon to help other people find this book too.